LEARNER-CENTERED TEACHING

LEARNER-CENTERED TEACHING

Putting the Research on Learning Into Practice

Terry Doyle

Foreword by Todd Zakrajsek

1996–2011 15TH ANNIVERSARY

Stylus
PUBLISHING, LLC.

STERLING, VIRGINIA

COPYRIGHT © 2011 BY
STYLUS PUBLISHING, LLC.

Published by Stylus Publishing, LLC
22883 Quicksilver Drive
Sterling, Virginia 20166-2102

Library of Congress Cataloging-in-Publication Data
Doyle, Terry, 1951-
    Learner-centered teaching : putting the research on
learning into practice / Terry Doyle ; foreword by Todd
Zakrajsek.
        p.   cm.
    Includes bibliographical references and index.
    ISBN 978-1-57922-742-5 (cloth : alk. paper)
    ISBN 978-1-57922-743-2 (pbk. : alk. paper)
    ISBN 978-1-57922-744-9 (library networkable e-edition)
    ISBN 978-1-57922-745-6 (consumer e-edition)
    1. Student-centered learning.   2. Active learning.
3. Effective teaching.   I. Title.
LB1027.23.D69   2011
370.15′4—dc23   2011016318

13-digit ISBN: 978-1-57922-742-5 (cloth)
13-digit ISBN: 978-1-57922-743-2 (paper)
13-digit ISBN: 978-1-57922-744-9 (library networkable
e-edition)
13-digit ISBN: 978-1-57922-745-6 (consumer e-edition)

Printed in the United States of America

All first editions printed on acid-free paper
that meets the American National Standards Institute
Z39-48 Standard.

Bulk Purchases

Quantity discounts are available for use in workshops
and for staff development.
Call 1-800-232-0223

First Edition, 2011

10   9   8   7   6   5   4   3   2

For Jessica and Brendan,
my two lovers of learning!

CONTENTS

ACKNOWLEDGMENTS

I want to begin by thanking my amazing wife, Professor Julie Doyle, for the endless hours she listened to me as I talked about what I was trying to do in this book. I also want to thank her for the many suggestions she gave, especially in chapter 5, on how to build relationships with students that lead to better learning. This is an area where she is an expert.

I want to thank the hundreds of faculty members I have talked with on campuses and at conferences over the past 15 years as I worked to become a more learner-centered teacher. Their questions, insights, and support for my work inspired me to write this book. I want to thank all of my friends at LILLY, especially Milt Cox, Laurie Richland, Gregg Wentzell, Jim Eisner, Barbara Millis, and Ron Berk, who have shared their ideas about teaching and learning with me. In particular, I want to acknowledge my friend Todd Zakrajsek, who wrote the foreword to this book.

I want to thank Michael Graham Richard for allowing me to use his fine work on mindset in chapter 5, Robert Barkman for allowing me to use his excellent work on patterns in chapter 9, and Marilyn Lombardi for her work on authentic learning that appears in chapter 3.

I am particularly grateful to my editor Karyn Bledsoe for her outstanding work in helping me to be clear and concise as I worked to explain my ideas about teaching and learning, and to John von Knorring at Stylus for providing me an outlet to share my ideas about learner-centered teaching with the higher education community.

Finally, I want to thank Ferris State University for granting me the sabbatical leave that allowed me to complete this book in a timely manner and my many students, who give me inspiration and from whom I have learned so much about how to be a learner-centered teacher.

FOREWORD

Placed before a class and given the constraints of a specific area of content, college and university educators have the very difficult task of intellectually advancing everyone in the room as far as possible within a very limited amount of time. The typical instructor has to determine quickly the extent to which each student has the appropriate foundational knowledge, the best way to present the material, how the students should interact with and use the content, and what methods will be used to assess the extent to which the students have learned that which was desired to be taught. Few faculty members are taught how best to accomplish all of this, and without that knowledge they are forced to engage in pedagogical mimicry—teaching the same way their best teachers taught them. Although this approach may work at a rudimentary level, it does not build on the very real advances that have taken place in teaching and learning. It also results in each succeeding educational generation facing the same challenges.

Unless instructors take a pedagogy course or some other form of educational training so they do not have to rely solely on a foundation of mimicry, the most common method to advance teaching skills is through trial and error. Trial and error is problematic for several reasons. First, it does not allow one to understand why some approaches work and others fail. Even when strategies are discovered that work well, it is unlikely this new strategy will be transferred successfully to future teaching challenges if there is no understanding about why the methodology was successful. I have met many faculty colleagues with strong opinions regarding the teaching strategies they use, but they have no clear understanding about why these strategies work or don't work in their classes. As a result, these individuals see each teaching challenge as a unique experience that must be solved by a trial-and-error approach. A second concern with trial and error is that it does not allow the field of teaching and learning to advance. I frequently work with faculty members who, without realizing the extent of current relevant pedagogical research, decided to try using groups in class, have heard about active learning and wanted to give it a try, or are currently attempting to better engage and motivate students in the learning process. Without consulting current research, simply trying new approaches in class is unlikely to result in any meaningful advances in how we teach and how students learn, any more than it would advance any discipline. As an example, it would be most disconcerting if a social psychologist decided that she was going to determine the effects of giving two different groups instructions with varying levels of specificity to see which would result in the best completed project if she did not consult at least some of the relevant literature.

Although consulting the relevant literature is important in advancing any area of study, when that literature is outside one's area of expertise, it is difficult to know where to begin. In addition, disciplinary research is often written in area-specific jargon that makes it difficult to understand the findings *and* use the results in a meaningful way. That is specifically why, through this book, *Learner-Centered Teaching: Putting the Research on Learning Into Practice*, Terry Doyle has made such an important contribution to the field of teaching and learning. The foundation of this book, which is consistent with all of Terry's work, is in helping higher education faculty members better understand how to assist college and university students to learn. He uses up-to-date research in the field of teaching and learning as a foundation, and he does so without using jargon. It is becoming increasingly common to find faculty members who understand that engaged active learning is the best way for students to acquire new knowledge. These same faculty members are fully willing to augment, or even give up, the standard lecture. The major challenge for them is to understand which of the pedagogical approaches currently being advocated have an empirical foundation and which are based on speculation. That is, their challenge is to find the relevant literature.

Terry Doyle states clearly in this book the importance of "following the research" on teaching and learning. Following his advice minimizes the dangers of using seemingly commonsense practices that might actually hinder learning. Throughout this book, Terry summarizes the evidence pertaining to learning that is both accessible and readily applicable. He includes many suggested strategies and multiple examples to assist faculty members in using the material presented. To me, the greatest value of this book is the way in which Terry pulls together research pertaining to the most common challenges with respect to teaching and learning that most faculty members face but have had no time to research on their own. For example, speaking from his experience as a primary school teacher, Terry notes that what is often common to every grade school teacher, lesson planning, is often not even on the radar of college and university faculty members. In addition, based on his extensive university teaching experience and faculty development workshops, he presents empirically based findings in areas such as getting students to understand the value of participatory learning, emphasizing authentic learning, better understanding who is in your class, facilitating discussion, and how the brain best retains and recalls information. These are presented in elegantly understandable descriptions of the major findings.

Why is a book titled *Learner-Centered Teaching: Putting the Research on Learning Into Practice* so very important to those who teach at the college and university level? Understanding pedagogical research and the implications for helping college and university students to be successful is extremely important in educating our next generation of leaders. Teaching is not something that should be left to trial and error, and it certainly should not be done without building on an understanding of what is already known about this vital activity. Perhaps our biggest challenge in convincing ourselves and others of the importance of following the research is that both teaching and learning are elusive and difficult because they appear to be such common-sense, innate activities. Essentially all humans, without any specific training, are capable both of teaching others and of learning from them. Ask a person on the street for directions, and she quickly provides them; offer your opinion on a dining establishment and friends will choose to eat there or not, based on what they have learned from you. That which is commonly done without specialized training seems not to need specialized training. The general belief that teaching at the postsecondary level requires no disciplinary expertise in pedagogy is evidenced by the fact that there is almost no certification or demonstration of competence before allowing an individual to teach in higher education in the United States (though not so in some European countries). Disciplines are given prestige based on the real or perceived special knowledge needed to be successful. Teaching is a profession that does require special skills and knowledge to maximize what students can learn, and it should be taken much more seriously than it is today. Regular reference to and inclusion of research on effective teaching strategies and how people learn will help our current students and advance those same teaching strategies in the future, as well as make our lives as teachers progressively easier and more enjoyable. This book is an important contribution because it provides a starting place for those who would like to better understand how best to help students learn. The evidenced-based approaches suggested throughout this book do just that.

Todd Zakrajsek
Executive Director, Center for Faculty Excellence
University of North Carolina at Chapel Hill

INTRODUCTION

I have had the honor of working with faculty members on more than 60 college campuses over the past 7 years, and I have spoken at another 50 or so regional, national, and international conferences on topics related to learner-centered teaching (LCT). Most of the faculty members I have met on these occasions were very interested in improving their teaching and moving toward a more learner-centered practice. I have found, however, that their hearts are willing, but their skill sets are often lacking.

Learner-Centered Teaching: Putting the Research on Learning Into Practice

I have written this book in the hope of providing my colleagues in higher education the specific skills and strategies needed to move away from a teacher-centered lecture model of instruction to a learner-centered model of facilitating learning. Neuroscience, biology, and cognitive science research have made it clear that the one who does the work does the learning. Many faculty members do too much of the work for their students, which results in diminished student learning.

In my first book on learner-centered teaching, I addressed the issue that students were being asked to make significant changes in how they approached learning in a learner-centered course but were not being taught how to make these changes. Students were expected to take on new learning responsibilities and actions without having the skills necessary to do so. I wrote that if this significant gap between what students were used to doing in school and what a learner-centered teacher required them to do was not closed, it would mean failure for the learner-centered approach. My message was simple: We must teach our students how to learn in a learner-centered environment because no one else will. I believe similar problems exist for faculty members: They face a gap between what they would like to do in their teaching and the skills and strategies they need to make it happen.

I define learner-centered teaching as making decisions about what and how students will learn based on one question. Given the context of your teaching (number of students, time of day, classroom configuration, and so on), how will your instructional decisions optimize the opportunity for students to learn the skills and content of the course? In other words, are the activities you've chosen for class today the best possible for students to learn the skills and content of the course? The question sounds simple enough, but arriving at an accurate answer involves an understanding of current brain research on cognition and learning, knowledge of various pedagogical approaches and strategies to improve students' comprehension and recall, recognition of the affective concerns of students, the design of effective assessment strategies, successful communication techniques, and other essential matters that surround the learning process. I address all of these issues in this book.

The purpose of this book, *Learner-Centered Teaching: Putting the Research on Learning Into Practice*, is to make a research-based case supporting learner-centered teaching as the best approach for optimizing the opportunity for college students to learn. The book grew out of recognition that many in higher education still do not understand or accept the scientific findings that demonstrate LCT optimizes student learning. For example, when considering the file of a faculty member who is a strong advocate and user of learner-centered practice for a Teacher of the Year award, a colleague of mine commented that he and his other colleagues "don't do that learner-centered teaching stuff" in their program. Three things struck me about this statement. First, it was a statement admitting to a fear of change. Second, it was a statement of defiance (How dare anyone question what I have been doing for 20 years in my classes!). Third, it was a statement of ignorance. I say ignorance because this faculty member's program engages students in all kinds of authentic learning experiences; it uses authentic, problem-based learning in classes and the students do a great deal of collaborative work. These are categorically learner-centered practices! It is my belief that many of my colleagues who fear a change to a learner-centered practice are actually much closer to being learner-centered teachers than they think; they just don't understand what LCT is all about.

It is my hope that this book will promote discussions on campuses about the use of LCT. I sincerely hope faculty members will recognize that LCT is not some radical new pedagogy; rather, it is a practice that keeps all of the good features from the teacher-centered approach and applies them in ways that are in better harmony with how our brains learn. For example, learner-centered teaching embraces the teacher as expert as well as the appropriate use of lecture, both of which are features of the teacher-centered approach. At the same time, it offers new, effective ways to replace the characteristics of teacher-centered instruction that were not optimizing student learning.

What Will You Learn in This Book?

I have designed this book so that each chapter can be a stand-alone lesson on learner-centered teaching. Each chapter addresses a different question about how to move our teaching to a more learner-centered practice. These questions came from faculty members I have worked with across the higher education spectrum, both in the United States and around the world. I believe these questions reflect the general concerns of most higher education teachers who are seeking to optimize their students' learning. I will describe each chapter in more detail than others might do in a book's introduction so that readers who are looking for specific strategies or skills can go directly to that specific chapter.

Chapter 1, "Follow the Research," addresses the question, What does the research from neuroscience, biology, cognitive psychology, and, most recently, evolutionary biology say about how human brains learn, and what is the application of these findings to teaching and learning in higher education? The chapter summarizes the brain research findings of the past 15 years that have application to teaching and learning. The main finding is that the one who does the work does the learning. If students are to learn, then it must be their brains that do the work. We must be the designers and facilitators of that work.

Chapter 2, "Getting Students to Do the Work," discusses the question, How can we get the students to do the work? It looks at the reasons why students might not like doing more work. A student who has had success in a teacher-centered classroom for 12 years is not always excited to encounter a new model where he or she can no longer sit passively and listen but instead must play a much more active role in his or her learning.

Chapter 3, "The Power of Authentic Learning," responds to those who wonder, How do we engage students in authentic learning experiences that model the real world of work they will enter when they graduate?" How do we come up with the kinds of experiences that authentic learning expert Jon

Mueller says move students from learning about history, biology, or math to actually doing history, biology, or math? Authentic learning experiences address the students' question, How am I going to use this in the real world? Authentic learning is about getting students to apply their knowledge in meaningful ways that lead to solving real-world problems. Chapter 3 also includes ways to assess students' learning by using authentic tools that reflect how students will be expected to use their skills and knowledge in the workplace and in their lives.

Chapter 4, "From Lecturer to Facilitator," looks at the process involved in moving our role in teaching from that of a teller of knowledge to a facilitator of learning. The biggest challenge faculty members face when moving from a teacher-centered or lecture-oriented instructional approach to a learner-centered one is figuring out how to stop talking and still have students learn something. Most of us who teach in higher education came through a very teacher-centered, lecture-oriented educational system that had an authoritarian design and unisensory approach to teaching. This is not an ideal teaching model to copy, given what we now know from the last 15 years of research on how humans learn. In addition, many of us had little formal instruction in pedagogy and, if we did, it was in how to lecture effectively. As a result, we do not have a toolkit full of the skills needed to be a facilitator of learning, despite our desire to become one. Chapter 4 lays out a step-by-step approach to becoming a facilitator of learning and focuses on the vital importance of lesson planning. Lesson planning, according to my long-time colleague, Dr. Kitty Manley, is 80% of effective teaching.

In chapter 5, "Who Are Our Learners and How Do We Get to Know Them Better?" I make the case that we must have a deeper understanding of who our students are and how they learn and study best if we are to optimize our students' learning, which is at the heart of learner-centered teaching. Chapter 5 examines Carol Dweck's work on students' mindsets. To be effective in our teaching, it is crucial to know what kind of mindset our students have (fixed or growth) and how to help students with a fixed mindset develop a growth mindset. Carol Dweck has produced more than 30 years of research findings that clearly show that a student's mindset has a profound impact on his or her learning. Chapter 5 then looks at the research on relationship-driven teaching. This research demonstrates the powerful role emotional connections play in enhancing students' learning. Specific strategies for building trusting and meaningful relationships with students and rationales for why these relationships enable learner-centered teaching to thrive are discussed.

Chapter 6, "Sharing Control and Giving Choices," considers the question, How can we successfully share power with our students? Sharing power is one of the most important aspects of learner-centered teaching and the one that usually makes faculty members the most uncomfortable. I make the case that, in sharing power (by giving up some control and offering students learning choices), we are enhancing learning by leading to improved engagement in the learning process. A sense of personal control is a constant desire of humans. Its absence brings a loss of a sense of well-being, which in turn hinders learning. Chapter 6 also addresses specific ways of giving students a variety of learning choices that can enhance motivation, boost interest, and maximize learning.

In chapter 7, "How Teachers Can Facilitate Student Discussions by Not Talking," I ask the question, If multiple brains almost always outperform single brains, which research clearly says is true, then why is discussion the least-used learning tool in higher education? National studies indicate that only 1% to 3% of classroom time is spent in discussion. Ironically, our students will spend more of their professional lives talking and listening to people than doing any other activity. Chapter 7 examines how to incorporate more discussion into instruction. I suggest ways to let students have input on the formation and execution of classroom discussions, who leads the discussions, who authors the topics for discussion, and how the rubrics are designed to evaluate discussions. In addition, chapter 7 looks at issues surrounding the development of discussion groups, pairs, and large-group discussions. It also includes specific suggestions for when and how teachers should get involved in classroom discussions.

Chapter 8, "Teaching to All the Senses," discusses research findings that answer this question: How do human senses affect teaching and learning? It explores research that shows, when multiple senses are used in learning, the senses work together to boost the overall learning process. Chapter 8 focuses on how to teach using multiple sensory techniques, especially those of visual experiences because vision exceeds all other senses in its importance to learning. The chapter also suggests ways to help students use more of their senses to improve their learning.

In chapter 9, "Patterns: A Major Element in Effective Teaching and Learning," I explore the research findings showing the brain to be a pattern-seeking device that relates whole concepts to one another and looks for similarities, differences, or relationships between them (Ratey, 2001, p. 5). Every subject area has its own patterns. These patterns represent the specific ways in which the information is ordered or organized. Chapter 9 investigates the patterns in a multitude of content areas and offers teachers ways to teach in harmony with the patterns of their subject matter. It also supplies specific suggestions for teachers who ask, How can I help my students use patterns to enhance their learning?

In chapter 10, "Repetition and Elaboration," I examine the memory research that shows two major factors in effective long-term recall. One is that the information must be repeated over time. The other is that recall is much easier if the information is elaborated upon. Chapter 10 discusses the work of John Medina, John Ratey, Robert Bjork, Janet Zadina, and Daniel Schacter in the effort to answer the question, How does the brain make memories and how can we teach and help our students learn to study in ways that promote long-term recall?

In chapter 11, "Is a Revolution Coming? Movement, Exercise, and Learning," I explore the research findings from evolutionary biology that strongly indicate humans were meant to move while learning, not sit at desks. In Harvard professor John Ratey's 2008 book, *Spark the Revolutionary New Science of Exercise and the Brain,* he said that exercise is the single most important thing a person can do to improve learning. Chapter 11 answers the question, Why do movement and exercise help learning and what are some creative ways we can get more movement in our classes?

Chapter 12, "Getting Others to Embrace Learner-Centered Teaching," addresses the question most frequently asked by faculty members: How do I justify my use of a learner-centered practice when my department chair or colleagues don't support it? Chapter 12 outlines specific arguments that give strong support to LCT and offers a set of actions to defend and advocate for a learner-centered practice. I have found that many people who oppose LCT actually know very little about it. The chapter is designed to educate them and support this research-based, authentic approach to improved student learning.

Additionally, chapters 1, 4, 8, 9, and 10 have related videos. The videos can be viewed on video enabled e-readers or accessed on-line at tinyurl.com/learnercenterdvideo.

Learner-centered teaching is the first teaching approach based on hard science. It represents a new paradigm in how we look at the teaching process. As a relentless explorer of the best ways to help students learn, I have seen research prove again and again that LCT is the most powerful enhancement for student learning. By reading this book and trying the suggestions you find here, you are demonstrating that you, too, desire to cultivate the potential of your students by serving them in a way supported by modern scientific research. With the skill set and knowledge necessary for moving forward, you'll be a practicing advocate of the learner-centered teaching approach.

FOLLOW THE RESEARCH

Whole swaths of the brain not only turn on, but
also get functionally connected when you're
actively exploring the world.

(as cited in Nauert 2010)

The question everyone asks, and rightly so, is, Why should teachers change to a learner-centered approach to instruction? The answer is actually very simple. Fifteen years of neuroscience, biology, and cognitive psychology research findings on how humans learn offer this powerful and singular conclusion: "It is the one who does the work who does the learning" (Doyle, 2008). This conclusion strongly suggests that the traditional model of teacher-centered instruction, where teachers do a lot of the work, is less effective and can be detrimental to students' learning. Therefore, a new approach is needed that gets the students to do most of the learning work, and that approach is learner-centered teaching.

The One Who Does the Work Does the Learning

Learner-centered teaching (LCT) is about optimizing the opportunities for our students to learn. This means figuring out the best possible ways to get them to do the work. The widely accepted definition of learning is that it is a change in neuron-networks of the brain (Goldberg, 2009; Ratey, 2001). For this change to happen, students must be paying attention and actively engaging their brains to process new sensory input. There is no such thing as passive learning. Cognitive neuroscientist Janet Zadina explained in her presentations that, if students' brains are engaged in new learning, their brains' neurons (specifically the dendrites) begin to grow new cellular material. This new material is the start of new neural connections that will represent the new information. She also pointed out that if the new information

---

To view chapter-related videos please go to tinyurl.com/learnercenteredvideo.

does not get used or practiced, the brain will reabsorb the new cellular material. Zadina made it clear that the brain is good at conserving its resources. Therefore, the only way for our students to increase their learning is to actively engage in learning the content and skills we teach, and then use and practice the content and skills for significant periods of time. This practice causes the new neural connections to grow into permanent representations of the learned material. This means that most of the time, our students need to be doing more than just listening to a lecture. Our students need to be doing the work.

In their new book, *Academically Adrift: Limited Learning on College Campuses,* Arum and Roksa (2011) used the Collegiate Learning Assessment (CLA) test to show that after two years of college, students haven't learned very much. Forty-five percent of the 3,000 students in the study showed no significant gains in learning after 2 years, and 36% showed little change after 4 years. The CLA does not measure content gains, just core outcomes, including critical thinking, analytical reasoning, problem solving, and writing. The reasons for these poor results are tied directly to the amount of time spent in learning and the amount of work students were asked to do. Students reported that they spent on average only 7% of their time each week studying compared to 51% socializing. Thirty-five percent of students said that they spend five or fewer hours each week studying on their own, and those who spent additional study time in groups tended to have lower gains in learning. Fifty percent of the students said that, in a typical semester-long course, they wrote less than 20 pages, and 32% said that they had to read no more than 40 pages per week (Arum & Roksa, 2011). Although this is only one study, and some professionals in higher education are questioning some aspects of the study, these findings speak loudly to the need for getting our students to do more of the work, which is a goal of learner-centered teaching.

A Clarification About the Use of Lecture

Before moving on, an important clarification about learner-centered practice and the use of lecture must be made. Lecture has an important place in a learner-centered practice. Students will always need teachers to explain complex and complicated information and to give great examples to help connect new information to students' backgrounds. This remains a vital role for faculty members. However, the use of lecture in a learner-centered practice needs to follow a simple definition; lecture is talking to students about things they can't learn on their own. When seeking to optimize students' learning, teachers must make careful decisions in determining when students need to listen and when they need to try to figure things out on their own. Chapter 8 discusses ways to make lecture a more effective teaching tool by making it a multisensory experience for the students.

The Goal of LCT

The goal of a learner-centered practice is to create learning environments that optimize students' opportunities to pay attention and actively engage in authentic, meaningful, and useful learning. This kind of learning activates the reward pathway in the brain that is responsible for driving our feelings of motivation, reward, and behavior. The reward pathway releases the chemical dopamine, which gives us a little jolt of pleasure, enticing us to repeat the behavior (Genetics Science Learning Center, 2010). Activating this pathway is a major key to successful learning (Zadina, 2010). It is a bit ironic that the more "helpful" a teacher is in terms of giving students answers or solving their problems, the less the students actually learn. I say "ironic" because the very thing many students want their teachers to do and that many teachers *like* to do is provide solutions to educational exercises. This may be why teacher-centered instruction has persisted for centuries and continues to be a regular practice within higher education today. It makes everyone happy. But just because everyone is "happy" doesn't make it an effective pedagogy.

An Obligation to Follow Where the Brain Research Leads—A Personal Experience

In 1995, I read *A Celebration of Neurons* by University of Oregon education professor Robert Sylwester. This was the first book I had ever read about the human brain and learning. One of the first points Dr. Sylwester made in this book was that the information on which we base our teaching decisions is much closer to folklore than science. This bit of wisdom confronted me in the most powerful way when, in 2009, French neuroscientist Stanislas Dehaene wrote a book titled *Reading in the Brain*. As a reading teacher by training, I was eager to find out what neuroscience had discovered about the reading process. What I discovered caused me not only to rethink my approach to teaching reading, but to cringe at the advice I had given over the years to many of my students who suffered from dyslexia.

For over a century, it had been assumed that dyslexia was a problem in the visual-processing area of the human brain. This assumption was plausible because a common symptom that someone suffering from dyslexia has is difficulty in recognizing words in the correct pattern. For example, a person with dyslexia would see *was* as *saw*. For a hundred years, The Orton Society has dedicated itself to helping people with dyslexia based on the belief that dyslexia is a visual-processing problem. However, Dehaene made it very clear that brain research *indicates* dyslexia is in fact an auditory-processing problem (Dehaene, 2009). Specifically, dyslexia appears to be a reading deficit that can be reduced to a problem with single word decoding, which is itself due to impairment in grapheme-phoneme conversion. Put another way, it is a problem in speech processing (Dehaene, 2009, p. 239). How could so many well-meaning teachers and reading experts get it so wrong? Brain-imaging tools that show what is really happening in the brains of people suffering from dyslexia had not yet been available. The best guesses were just that: guesses. And those guesses were wrong. The exciting part about these wrong guesses is that because of them, we now know the brain is so malleable and has so many redundant systems, especially in children, it may be possible to design training programs that teach children to use other brain systems to overcome some of the problems dyslexia presents (Dehaene, 2009, p. 258)!

Dehaene also taught me a second powerful lesson. I have always been a firm believer in a whole language approach to teaching reading, ever since I read Indiana University professor Frank Smith's book *Reading Without Nonsense* in 1985. Smith emphasized that learners need to focus on meaning and strategy instruction, and that language is treated as a complete meaning-making system, with the parts functioning in relational ways. The goal was to immerse students in the reading process with the belief that they would, through repeated exposure, acquire the reading skills they needed to be successful. Phonics was seen as slowing readers down. However, as Dr. Dehaene pointed out, brain research does not support a whole language approach. Research findings show phonics is necessary because of how it changes the way the brain processes speech sounds. This finding means that the crucial process by which written words are turned into strings of phonemes must be explicitly taught. How the brain processes speech sounds doesn't happen just from immersion into language. Such findings from neuroscience research required me to reconsider my approach with students who were seriously limited in their reading abilities. I now include instruction in phonics activities. If I am to optimize my students' learning, I need to follow the research.

Another example of the power of moving from folklore to science comes from the work of Dr. Aditi Shankardass. Dr. Shankardass is a neuroscientist trained across three disciplines of the field: neurophysiology, neuroanatomy, and neuropsychology. Currently, she leads the Neurophysiology Lab of the Communicative Disorders Department at California State University. Dr. Shankardass's work has been devoted to the use of an advanced form of digital quantitative electroencephalography (EEG) technology that records the brain's activity in real time and then analyzes it using complex display schematics and statistical comparisons to norms, thus enabling far more accurate diagnoses of children with developmental disorders. Dr. Shankardass reported that as many as 50% of the people diagnosed with autism and other developmental disorders have been misdiagnosed. Some children diagnosed with autism are actually suffering from micro brain seizures that produce the same symptoms as autism but can be treated with medication (Shankardass, 2009). Dr. Shankardass's work provides a powerful example of how many of our current assumptions about the best ways to help students learn may actually restrict their potential. We who teach in higher education, especially because we have been trained to be researchers, have an obligation to follow where the research leads us.

What Can Brain Research Tell Us About Students' Learning?

First, Be Cautious About the Information

Essential information about the brain comes from biologists who study brain tissue, experimental psychologists who study behavior, and cognitive neuroscientists who study how the first relates to the second (Medina, 2008). The relationship between brain systems and complex cognition and behavior can only be explained satisfactorily by a comprehensive blend of theories and facts related to all the levels of organization of the nervous system, from molecules and cells and circuits, to large-scale systems and physical and social environments. We must beware of explanations that rely on data from one single level, whatever the level may be (Damasio, 2001).

Neuroscientist Peter Snyder of Brown University cautioned in a 2010 *Newsweek* article that lots of quick and dirty studies of cognitive enhancement make the news, but the number of rigorous, well-designed studies that stand the test of time is much smaller. Further, he wrote, "It's kind of the wild, wild west right now" (as cited in Begley, 2011). Almost daily, we see reports on something new that can make us smarter or keep our brains younger or healthier. The facts are often quite different. For example, in the 2010 evaluation of purported ways to maintain or improve cognitive function, conducted for the National Institutes of Health, vitamins B6, B12, E, beta-carotene, folic acid, and the trendy antioxidants called flavenoids were all found to be busts when it comes to enhancing cognition. Findings that alcohol and omega-3 fatty acids (the fatty acids in fish) and having a large social network enhance cognition were found to be weak. Research on the value of statins found they do not enhance cognition, and neither does estrogen or nonsteroidal anti-inflammatory drugs (NSAIDs; aspirin, ibuprofen). Snyder also suggested in the *Newsweek* article that we be skeptical of practices that promise to make us smarter by increasing blood flow to the brain: There is no evidence that more than normal blood flow would be of value to the brain.

What Do We Know? We Can Get Smarter!

Neuroscientist James Bibb of the University of Texas was an organizer of a symposium on "Cognitive Enhancement Strategies" at the 2010 meeting of the Society for Neuroscience. He said, "Neuroscientists have accumulated enough knowledge about the mechanisms and molecular underpinnings of cognition at the synaptic and circuit levels to say something about which processes contribute to cognitive enhancement" (as cited in Begley, 2011). What are cognitive enhancements? They are behaviors, drugs, nutrients, or other stimuli that help the brain produce more neurons or synapses and create higher levels of neurogenesis (the growth of new neurons), especially in the memory-forming hippocampus. They also increase production of brain derived neurotrophic factor (BDNF), which stimulates the production of neurons and synapses. Neurogenesis and synapse formation boost learning, memory, reasoning, and creativity. For example, people that excel at a particular task have more synapses, thus causing their brain circuits to be more efficient (using less energy even as cognitive demand increases), with higher capacity, and to be more flexible (Begley, 2011).

Neuroplasticity

One of the most important research findings for educators about the human brain is the neuroplasticity of the brain. Neuroplasticity refers to the ability of the human brain to change by adding new neural connections and to grow new neurons as a result of one's experience. This is the proof that the one who does the work does the learning. These increases in neural connections and new neurons are what neuroscientists say make us smarter.

The information that the brain actively pays attention to is the key to new neural growth. For example, skills we've already mastered don't make us much smarter because we barely pay attention to them. However, new, cognitively demanding activity such as learning a foreign language or taking an economics course for the first time is more likely to boost processing speed, strengthen synapses, and expand or create functional networks (Begley, 2011). We have always known that we have to have our students' attention to teach them; this finding reinforces that working knowledge.

Another area of interest to educators is cognitive training. A significant number of new businesses have been developed on the belief that engaging the brain in cognitive training boosts mental prowess, and studies show this is true. However, memory training, reasoning, or speed of processing improves only the particular skill on which it is focused and does not generalize to other tasks (Stern, 2009). In other words, doing crossword puzzles just makes you better at doing crossword puzzles. Scientists are most interested in activities or drugs that actually boost overall memory, reasoning ability, or speed of processing.

What Else Do We Know?

Daydreaming and Attention

I still remember how upset the nuns I had in grade school would get with students who daydreamed. They saw daydreaming as a sign of being a "slacker." I can't help but wonder what they would think of the following studies. Studies on mind wandering show that all people find it difficult to stay focused for more than a few minutes on even the easiest tasks, despite the fact that we make mistakes whenever we drift away (Smallwood & Schooler, 2006). Recent research shows that mind wandering can be positive because it allows us to work through some important thinking. Our brains process information to reach goals, but some of those goals are immediate and others are distant. Somehow, we have evolved a way to switch between handling the here and now and contemplating long-term objectives (Smallwood & Schooler, 2006). It may be no coincidence that most of the thoughts that people have during mind wandering have to do with the future. Even more telling is the discovery that "zoning out" may be the most fruitful type of mind wandering. Studies using functional magnetic resonance imaging (fMRI) found that the default network and executive control systems are even more active during zoning out than they are during the less extreme mind wandering with awareness. When we are no longer even aware that our minds are wandering, we may be able to think most deeply about the big picture (Smallwood & Schooler, 2006).

Multitasking and Learning

It is almost like a badge of honor to say that you are a multitasker in today's world. It's kind of like being the superman of brain power. The only problem is that multitasking is not possible when it comes to activities that require the brain's attention (Foerde, Knowlton, & Poldrack, 2006). Given that attention is the key to learning, this is a very important finding. Multitasking violates everything scientists know about how memory works. Imaging studies indicate that the memory tasks and the distraction stimuli engage different parts of the brain and that these regions probably compete with each other (Foerde, Knowlton, & Poldrack, 2006). Our brain works hard to fool us into thinking it can do more than one thing at a time. But it can't. When trying to do two things at once, the brain temporarily shuts down one task while trying to do the other (Dux, Ivanoff, Asplund, & Marois, 2006).

Shifting Tasks

If instead we define multitasking as successfully dealing with situations that require performing multiple tasks, appropriately shifting attention, and prioritizing the tasks, then it would be accurate to say that many people have developed this skill. In fact many jobs demand successful multitaskers who can focus their attention on the task where attention is most needed at the moment, and then adapt to changes in task priority as they occur. It is this latter feature of multitasking that suggests a natural relationship with adaptive performance; the capability to adapt to changing task priorities is essential for effective complex task performance (Oberlander, Oswald, Hambrick, & Jones, 2007). Clearly the ability to switch tasks quickly is an important skill, and many of our students are good at it; however, even this form of multitasking has its drawbacks. Studies by University of Michigan neuroscientist Marc Berman show that processing a barrage of information leaves people mentally fatigued. Even though people feel entertained, even relaxed, when they are multitasking, they're actually fatiguing themselves (Berman & Kaplan, 2010). The drawback to brain fatigue is that our brains need to engage in direct attention to be in a learning mode. When the brain is fatigued, learning becomes much more difficult to accomplish. One solution is a walk in nature, which replenishes our capacity to attend and thus has a restorative effect on our mental abilities (Berman, Jonides, & Kaplan, 2008). Berman and Kaplan's work also found that irritability in people is often caused by brain fatigue. On days when our students are upset, perhaps it is just that their brains are tired.

Downtime and Learning

University of California at San Francisco neuroscientist Loren Frank found in a 2009 study that the brains of rats that were given downtime following new learning could solidify the new learning experiences and turn them into permanent, long-term memories while still awake. It had been the assumption that long-term memory formation happens only during sleep. Frank reported that when the brain is not given downtime, memory solidification and formation processes don't take place. He indicated in his study that he suspects the findings also apply to the process of human learning (Karlsson & Frank, 2009). A study in 2010 by neuroscientist Lila Davachi of New York University found that during rest following new learning, the areas of the brain that are active during learning remain just as active, especially if the task is particularly memorable. She indicated that the greater the correlation between rest and learning, the greater the chance of remembering the task in later tests. Davachi suggested in her study that taking a (coffee) break after class can actually help students retain the information they just learned. "Your brain is working for you when you're resting, so rest is important for memory and cognitive function" (as cited in Hamilton, 2010).

Drugs and Learning

When I present to faculty members that nicotine has been found to enhance attention, which is the key driver of neuroplasticity and cognitive performance in both smokers and nonsmokers, I have often received concerned responses ranging from, "Are you certain this is true?" to "I don't think this should be shared with our students." Despite the concerns, the National Institute on Drug Abuse (NIDA) reported in a 2010 analysis of 41 double-blind, placebo-controlled studies that nicotine has significant positive effects on fine motor skills, the accuracy of short-term memory, some forms of attention, and working memory, among other basic cognitive skills. The NIDA concluded that the improvements likely represent true performance enhancement and beneficial cognitive effects. The reason is that nicotine binds to the brain receptors for the neurotransmitter acetylcholine, which is a central player in cortical circuits (Begley, 2011). The findings also included a warning that smoking has been linked to dementia, among dozens of other health risks. Studies using nicotine in gum or patch form were not complete at the time of this writing.

Adderall and Ritalin

Stimulants such as Adderall and Ritalin have some cognitive benefits, at least in some people for some tasks. Studies show that both drugs enhance the recall of memorized words as well as working memory, which plays a key role in fluid intelligence (Begley, 2011). A survey done by McCabe, Knight, Teter, and Wechsler in 2005 estimated that almost 7% of students in U.S. universities had used prescription stimulants to aid learning and studying, and that on some campuses, up to 25% of students had used them in the past year. These two drugs, usually prescribed for people with attention deficit hyperactivity disorder (ADHD), increase executive functions both in people with ADHD and in most healthy people who do not have ADHD, improving their abilities to focus their attention, manipulate information in working memory, and flexibly control their responses (Sahakian & Morein-Zamir, 2007). It is important to note that use of prescribed medications by persons other than the patient is never recommended, and selling prescription drugs such as Adderall or Ritalin by a patient to others is a punishable violation of the law. I remind my students who do not have attention deficit disorder (ADD) or ADHD that 30 minutes of aerobic exercise (see chapter 11) will give them better attention and focus than these drugs, enhance their learning and memory, costs nothing, and won't cause them to break the law.

Three Cognitive Enhancements That Work

The three enhancements that have been very well tested and do show that they enhance cognitive function are exercise, especially aerobic exercise; meditation; and some computer games. I will discuss the important role that exercise can play in enhancing learning in chapter 11. The use of exercise to enhance learning is a very exciting finding and can have a significant impact on how we help students to learn and even how we conduct our classrooms.

Meditation can increase the thickness of brain regions that control attention and process sensory signals from the outside world (Jha, 2011). Meditation has shown success in enhancing mental agility and attention by changing brain structure and function so that brain processes are more efficient, a quality that is associated with higher intelligence (Jha, 2011). This finding is important to pass on to our students. Studies regarding the positive influence of meditation on the brain don't come only from neuroscience research. In fact, studies from other areas in health science have demonstrated positive health benefits from meditation such as lowered stress levels (Nidich et al., 2009).

Yaakov Stern, neuroscientist at Columbia University, found that some video games might improve general mental agility (as cited in Begley, 2011). Games that require motor control; visual search; working memory; long-term memory; decision making; and attention, specifically the ability to control and switch attention among different tasks, can enhance cognition. Only a limited number of games have been studied, but this research shows that people who play these types of video games are more successful on tests of memory, motor speed, visual-spatial skills, and cognitive flexibility.

Brain-Based Learning Has Arrived

Certainly one significant sign that higher education has begun to embrace the integration of neuroscience findings into teaching and learning is the establishment of a master's degree in Mind, Brain, and Education at Harvard University. Harvard's mission is to build a movement in which cognitive science and neuroscience are integrated into education so that educators will learn how to incorporate them both in research and practice.

Evolution and Learning

One of the most important things to recognize about the human brain comes from the study of human evolution. Natural selection favored a brain that could solve problems related to survival in an unstable outdoor environment, and to do so in nearly constant motion (Medina, 2008). The significance of this for educators is that it appears we have gotten the classroom model completely wrong. Students' brains evolved to work best when moving, not sitting. This finding brings new meaning to the idea of "active" learning. As discussed in further detail in chapter 11, a great deal of movement (aerobic exercise) is one of the best things our students can do to improve their learning.

Is it possible to teach students who are moving? Is this a better way for our students to do their work? At least in certain circumstances, the answer might be yes. Bob Nellis of the Mayo Clinic in Rochester, Minnesota, conducted a study on the benefits of "chairless classrooms" and found students to be more energetic and more engaged in this active learning environment. Students who needed movement were able to move, but they did so in ways that did not disturb others (Pytel, 2007). Across the United States, dozens of studies are underway in which desks have been replaced with tables and exercise or stability balls as chairs. When students sit on the balls, they have the freedom to move about in small but important ways. Research clearly indicates that movement, even in small amounts, is good for learning (Ratey, 2008). John Kilbourne, a professor in the Department of Movement Science at Grand Valley State University in Allendale, Michigan, switched to stability balls in his college courses in 2009. His survey of the 52 students in his class on the change from chairs to balls found that 98% of students preferred sitting on the balls. Students mentioned improvement in their ability to pay attention, focus, take notes, engage in classroom discussions, and take exams. "They said the balls improved their focus and their attention, that everything was just better" (Kilbourne, 2009).

In visiting campuses across the country, I regularly ask faculty how they might integrate more movement into their students' learning processes. I have received ideas ranging from holding moving discussion groups in which students are allowed to walk while discussing readings, to moving assessments in which students move about the room evaluating their peers' findings that have been posted on whiteboards or newsprint. If we are to optimize our students' opportunities to learn, then we need to put some creative thought into how movement may be integrated into courses, since this is where the research is leading us.

When Doing the Work, Two Heads Are Better Than One

The study of human evolution also provides strong evidence that human survival depends on humans working together. If humans didn't help each other adapt to new environments or solve new problems, they wouldn't have survived. Collaborating with others made survival possible. It was always better to have more than one person keeping an eye out for a hungry tiger or to have four people attack a mammoth rather than one. In keeping with the survival instinct, having students do their work in groups, teams, triads, or pairs has its origins in human evolution. The use of groups as a learner-centered learning tool is discussed in more detail in chapter 7. It is very helpful to share with students that collaborating is a natural part of who they are and that it continues to be important for their survival, in this case, their academic survival.

Try This Example

The following is a simple example to use with your students to illustrate the value of working and learning from others. Ask your students to add 17 and 55 together in their heads. Once they have done this task, survey the students for how they solved this simple cognitive problem. Ask how many added the numbers in columns, carrying the 1 to the 10's column, just like they would do on paper. Then ask how many added 10 to 55 to get 65 and then 7 to 65 to get 72. Finally, ask how many added 20 to 55 and subtracted 3 to get 72. You can also ask if anyone did the adding in a different way than the ones that are mentioned here. You'll find that sometimes you'll get some interesting answers. This exercise demonstrates that even with the simplest cognitive process, people don't think alike and don't use the same tools to get their answers. This means that there is often something to be learned by working with others. In this particular case, those who used columns could learn a more efficient system of computing the answer from the students who added 10 or added 20 and subtracted. In most cases, multiple brains outperform single brains (Medina, 2008).

Doing the Work Is the Way Our Students Make Long-Term Memories

As I mentioned earlier in the chapter, if our students' brains are going to develop new neural networks, they must use the new information and skills we teach for extended periods of time. This is necessary for the new networks to become well established and eventually permanent (Ratey, 2001). Without use and practice, the brain reabsorbs the new cellular material and no neural networks exist (Zadina, 2010). The application of this brain research finding to our teaching is clear. We must find ways to get our students to use and practice over time the new course material that we ask them to learn. Traditional methods of letting students listen passively to lectures and then use a short burst of intensive study to cram for a test three or four times a semester does not result in students forming new neural networks. Cramming does not result in the formation of long-lasting neural networks because the amount of time and number of practices needed for this process is completely inadequate (Medina, 2008, p. 125). UCLA psychologist and memory researcher Robert Bjork defined learning as "the ability to use information after significant periods of disuse and it is the ability to use the information to solve problems that arise in a context different (if only slightly) from the context in which the information was originally taught" (Bjork, 1994). By definition, a teaching approach that allows for cramming fails to meet the definition of learning. Cramming results in a hollow victory for students. They often earn a passing grade but they are unable to recall or use most of the information even a week later (Bjork, 1994; Ebbinghaus, 1913).

Each time our students use new information, their brains create stronger and faster connections for the neurons that represent that information (Ratey, 2008, p. 39). This is why it is so important to have students do a lot of the work in our courses. An equally important finding about long-term memory formation comes from the work of Harvard psychologist Daniel Schacter, in his book *The Seven Sins of Memory*. Dr. Schacter reported, "For better or worse, our recollections are largely at the mercy of our elaborations." If students are to form long-term memories, they need to use new information in a variety of ways (read, recode, write, summarize, annotate, speak, listen, map, reflect, etc.) to make the information available to them for recall through many different neural networks. In other words, they need to do a lot of work with the information to be able to recall it. In chapter 10, I take an in-depth look into the research of memory formation and recall and suggest applications of the research findings to instruction practices in ways that promote long-term recall.

Be Professionals by Following the Research

At a workshop in Oregon in 2010, I was asked what I thought about faculty members being evaluated on their teaching. I believe the question was posed because the person asking had a colleague who believed the administration was out to get rid of bad teachers by using evaluation practices. I answered that, "As professionals, we should be evaluated just like any other professional." I went on to say that we should welcome it as a way to improve our teaching and our students' learning. My message was that, as professional educators, we have the responsibility to maintain standards of practice and that this includes changing our teaching when the research offers evidence that new practices are warranted. We have an obligation to follow where the research leads us. As illustrated in this chapter, there is an extensive amount of research supporting the move to a learner-centered practice.

2

GETTING STUDENTS
TO DO THE WORK

Do not confuse motion and progress. A rocking
horse keeps moving but does not make any
progress.

(Alfred A. Montapert)

L ast winter, I had a small run-in with a student, call him KM, in one
of my study strategies courses. At the time, I had a faculty guest
visiting my classroom, so the brief confrontation had a heightened
drama to it. The conflict spurred from my request that KM remove his
headphones and listen to instructions. He first removed only one earbud, so
I asked him again. He then removed the other earbud but then pulled his
hat down over his eyes, apparently in protest. I politely asked him to raise
his hat and he replied in a highly disrespectful manner, "Get the f———
away from me!" Soon after the incident, I invited KM to my office to discuss
what had transpired. His first words to me were that I had caused it. He said
I had no business asking him to remove his earphones or raise his hat. I then
explained to him that one of the most important jobs I have as a teacher is
to maintain the learning environment of the classroom so that all students
can be fully prepared to engage in learning. I continued that his wearing of
earphones was an indication of a lack of readiness to learn, and it also sent a
message to other students that they could do the same. I explained that being
unprepared to learn was unacceptable and went against the whole purpose
of being in a college class. What happened next brings us to the point of this
story. KM told me that he had never heard that a teacher's job was to
maintain the learning environment or that teachers were supposed to make
students at least "appear" ready to learn. I told him that I was certain that
was my job and, in fact, I travel the country teaching other teachers that it

is one of the most important aspects of their jobs. He replied, "Well, I never heard of that before."

Why Our Students Might Not Like Doing the Work

My conversation with KM reminded me of why I wrote my first book on learner-centered teaching (LCT): because, to a great extent, I realized students were not ready for the new responsibilities and greater effort that LCT requires. In the first book, I wrote that students have very specific sets of ideas about how school is supposed to be based on their 12 or more years of being in school. When someone says those roles must change, which is exactly what happens when introducing a learner-centered practice, students often react in ways that are not accepting or even hostile. Twelve years is a long time to do something one way, especially when that way, for many of our students, has been rewarded with high grades and accolades.

Students often resist, at least initially, the roles and responsibilities that come with doing more of the work simply because this has never been asked of them before in a school setting. A teacher-centered practice simply requires less work from the students. Students can often go weeks without any assignment due or even a quiz to study for. Changing to a learner-centered practice, where work is due on a regular basis, where class time is spent trying to solve problems and figure out complex ideas instead of listening to a lecture, is a very different form of school. It's one that students need help adjusting to. As we all know, change can be difficult to accept.

K. Patricia Cross, one of the truly influential researchers on learning in higher education, spoke at a conference in 2001 about American students' views of effort; she said: "One of the oddities of traditional American culture, especially the youth culture, is that it is better to be thought lazy than stupid. Thus, in the competition of the classroom, students prefer to be seen by others as succeeding through ability rather than through effort" (Cross, 2001). In other words, students are inclined to think, "If I have to work at it, I must not be that smart." Learner-centered teaching requires more effort, and students aren't always ready for that new requirement.

Strategies for Letting Our Students Do the Work

Several chapters of this book detail ways to get students to do more of the work. But here are some quick and easy ways to start immediately getting students doing more of the work.

Cumulative Testing

In chapter 1, I discussed how practice is needed to form long-term memories. By forcing students to go back and relearn (and I do mean *relearn* in most cases rather than review previously tested material), we enhance the likelihood of our students meeting Robert Bjork's definition of learning: the ability to use information after periods of disuse. Several studies clearly show that cumulative testing is an excellent mechanism for improving long-term retention (Cull, 2000; McDaniel & Fisher, 1991; Pashler, Cepeda, Wixted, & Rohrer, 2005). These studies show that learning is often enhanced when the learner is required to recall information rather than simply restudy it (Roediger & Karpicke, 2006).

By focusing on the two or three most important points from each section of the course and retesting those points, you provide an effective mechanism for promoting long-term learning. A good way to look at this is to ask yourself, What would you most want your students to know and use a year after they completed your course? The answer is the material you should continually retest.

Establish a Wiki Site

One great way to help students do more of their own work is by establishing a wiki site or other appropriate online environment as a test review space for them. This online space lets students post course information, inquiries about course content, and possible test questions so everyone in the class can benefit. Because it is an open site, it can be monitored and material can be added or corrected. Basically it becomes the students' test review material. This online space also saves class time for other activities because an in-class test review is no longer needed.

Rewriting of Papers

Allow students to rewrite papers with the requirement that whatever suggested changes or corrections were made to their first paper must be visible in the rewrite. Rewriting is a powerful learning tool and clearly meets the goal of having the students do the work.

Retesting

Provide an opportunity to retest. Although it requires more time and effort for teachers, retesting prompts students to engage more fully with the course material. It is important to have students understand that there may be limits to the level of improvement that retesting can offer them. Here is an effective strategy: Allow the first test to determine 70% of the final grade, with the retest helping only with the remaining 30%. For example, if a student's score is 69% on a 100-point test, he or she earns 69% of the 70 points possible, which is 48 points. Even if he or she gets 100% of the 30 points available on the retests, his or her final grade will be 78/100.

Practice Quizzes

Faculty members have shared that one of the best methods to get students to do a lot of practicing is to provide them with test banks for practice quizzes on course material. More than 30 experimental studies have been done to measure the effect of this strategy for improving college students' academic performance. The findings repeatedly demonstrated that taking a test on studied material promotes remembering that material on a final test. Several recent studies have shown that testing not only enhances learning, it also reduces the rate at which information is forgotten (Chan, McDermott, & Roediger, 2007). Online delivery systems, such as Blackboard, are set up to allow this quizzing practice. Depending on the size of the test bank, students can take an endless number of quizzes and receive immediate feedback, which is a powerful way to study the course material.

Mapping

Chapter 8 discusses the power of using a multisensory approach to teaching and learning. An effective tool for this kind of learning is concept mapping. A valuable way to get students to do more of the work is to require them to make maps of their lecture notes and chapter readings. These maps will provide students with visual representations of the course ideas. Vision trumps all other senses when it comes to learning (Medina, 2008). Usually arranged in priority order from most to least important, the maps will represent the relationships between the ideas that are easy to miss in regular class notes or text materials.

A Scaffolding Approach to Getting Students to Do the Work

One of the crucial issues that teachers face in implementing a teaching model that gets students to do more work is ensuring that students have the skills and background knowledge they need to do the work while simultaneously not diminishing their learning by providing too much help. One solution comes from the research of Jean Piaget, Lev Vygotsky, and Jerome Bruner, three giants of psychology, in the form of the educational practice called scaffolding. Scaffolding in an educational context is a process by which a teacher provides students with a temporary framework for learning. Done correctly, such structuring encourages students to develop their own initiative, motivation, and resourcefulness. Once students build knowledge and develop skills on their own, elements of the framework are dismantled. Eventually, the initial scaffolding is removed altogether because students no longer need it (Smagorinsky, 2007). The defining features of successful scaffolding include providing students with clear direction, purpose, and expectation. Expected results include on-task activity; better student direction; reduced uncertainty, surprise, and disappointment; increased efficiency; and palpable momentum (McKenzie, 1999).

"Scaffolding requires continuous sorting and sifting as part of a 'puzzling' process—the combining of new information with previous understandings to construct new ones. Students are adding on, extending, refining and elaborating" (McKenzie, 1999). Students need enough help to get going and they need monitoring to see that their struggles are not overwhelming, but too much help and they won't struggle at all. For example, it does our muscles little good to lift the same weight the same amount of repetitions every day. Only when we struggle by adding weight do we begin to increase our strength.

Another important aspect of effective scaffolding is that our assistance results in the students seeing progress. James Zull, in his book *The Art of Changing the Brain* (2002), spoke about the important need for students to see that they are making some progress to sustain their efforts, especially in tasks that are difficult or that they don't like to do (Zull, 2002).

There are different models of scaffolding. One is an apprenticeship model whereby an expert models an activity, provides the student with advice and examples that guide the student in practice, and then tapers off support until the student can do the task alone (Lawson, 2002). A second model encourages ongoing use of tools and consultation with other people, arguing that in real life, few people ever work exclusively on their own (Bransford, Brown, & Cocking, 2000). Most agree that scaffolding is particularly effective in areas in which students need to be more self-reliant, such as technology-based learning (Banaszynski, 2000).

Zone of Proximal Development

A key element of successfully using a scaffolding approach is to determine the zone of proximal development (ZPD) in our students. First discussed by

Russian psychologist Lev Vygotsky, ZPD is the difference between what a learner can do without help and what he or she can do with help. Suppose a first-year student in a psychology course can read and understand the textbook material and some of the assigned outside readings from known experts that are explaining psychological research, but she cannot successfully read the research journal articles from psychology. We would say that the assigned outside readings are within her ZPD, and that this is the level at which assistance will be most profitable. "The instructional challenge is to provide problems that both fit the manner of the learner's thinking and tempt him/her into more powerful modes of thinking" (Perry, 2002).

Scaffolding and Math

A math instructional model that is quite popular uses a learner-centered scaffolding approach. Students are first placed through testing into the appropriate level of math course. The instruction process begins with allowing students to try and solve the assigned math problems on their own with no new instruction. The only instruction is what they had previously learned in other courses or, once a few days of class have transpired, what they learned in earlier parts of their current course. After trying on their own, students then work in pairs to help each other complete the problems. Finally, they work in groups of four and share their ideas and solutions. Once they have exhausted their own ideas, or in some cases discovered the answering process on their own, they ask questions of the teacher about the parts of the process they did not understand. The teacher answers all the questions and, if needed, engages in an instructional demonstration. In this model, support is given only when it is really needed. The specific need is usually clear because the students have made real efforts to learn the material on their own. Only when they could not understand the material was instruction provided (Yambric, 2008).

Let Students Try It on Their Own, With a Little Bit of Help

What is the best use of teachers' time in the classroom? This is a key question in a learner-centered practice. Is it best to explain concepts and ideas to everyone, even though some of our students can clearly figure them out on their own? If not, what do we do about those students who don't seem able to handle the learning tasks on their own? Will they fall far behind? Or should we first let all of our students try to do the work on their own with a little bit of help from us? Should we then follow this with having them work with each other to see if collaboration can resolve remaining difficulties, and then intercede only when they are having difficulties they can't resolve on their own or with peer assistance? While the correct action to take may depend on the learning situation, some instructional models clearly show the benefits of letting our students do the work on their own with just a little bit of help.

The Emporium Model

One very successful model is The Emporium Model of math instruction developed at Virginia Tech University. This model has been replicated at seven universities with significant success through the National Center for Academic Transformation (NCAT), Program in Course Redesign, which was funded by the Pew Charitable Trusts, 1999–2003. This model has demonstrated that it is possible to improve student learning by letting students first try to do the work on their own, with some software assistance to get them started, before any intervention from the teacher.

The Math Emporium Model:

- Uses computer technology to individualize a student's experience in a course, thus improving instruction. It allows students to progress at their own pace, review material, and take practice quizzes as much as they like. They can obtain personal help only when desired.
- Uses an active learning process as opposed to the traditional lecture model. The Emporium Model has improved learning when measured against traditional face-to-face learning.
- Uses faculty members and other coaches to provide just-in-time assistance 15 hours a day by using techniques designed to allow the students to discover answers themselves.
- Uses math courses that clearly delineate expectations and provides comfortable and effective mechanisms to support learning. However, students gain other valuable real-world skills beyond course content, including self-discipline and organization, when they are entrusted with the responsibility and authority to manage their own learning. These are the key elements of a learner-centered practice (Williams, 2005).

Here are some findings from the use of The Emporium Model:

- Enrolling 13,000 students annually, nine college-level math courses increased student success (final grade of C or better) by 25% on average, with a range of 7% to 63%.

- These same nine courses reduced the cost of instruction by 37% on average, with a range of 15% to 77%.
- Comparing grades of C or better most likely understates the achievements of The Emporium Model because grading standards under this model are higher and more consistent than under the traditional format, for example, no curves, no partial credit, consistent performance standards, and so on.

Clearly, the findings show that students can do a great deal of learning on their own, with proper assistance. It is interesting to note that, on one Virginia Tech student blog site, I found a student who hated The Emporium Model. His hatred was based on the fact that it required more work, more responsibility, and more initiative. He wrote, "For the students who are not independent learners, it is a terrible way to take a class." This is probably true. However, Americans now consume information for about 1.3 trillion hours each year, an average of almost 12 hours per day. Total information consumption totaled 3.6 zettabytes and 10,845 trillion words, with each person using, in some form, 34 gigabytes of information on an average day (Bohn & Short, 2009). In contrast, people living in the mid-1800s would have consumed in their lifetimes less information than is published in one week of the *New York Times*. The point is that students will need to become lifelong independent learners, whether they like it or not, if they hope to stay employed. Cognitive neuroscientist Janet Zadina put it this way: "Making learning too easy is a mistake."

We all can't develop interactive software that can help our students learn, but many companies are beginning to do just that. However, we all can understand the core of The Emporium Model, which is that students learned math by doing math. We all can put that kind of action into practice in our courses.

Sitting on My Stool

If you ever visit my classroom, you will likely find me sitting on my stool, watching my students engage in the day's learning activity. The reason I am just sitting and apparently not teaching is that I have already completed my work when I planned the activities that are now prompting my students to do their work. You might catch me doing a brief presentation, answering some questions, or debriefing the students following an activity, but in my classroom, students do the work. This is the goal of LCT. I am a facilitator of learning. This means my two main jobs are planning learning activities and giving students feedback. I discuss teacher as facilitator in more detail in chapter 4. My role is clearly different than what it was when I was a teacher-centered instructor. This new role takes some getting used to; however, each day I remind myself that I am following the research and I am optimizing my students' opportunities to learn. This is a responsibility all educators must accept.

3

THE POWER OF
AUTHENTIC LEARNING

From the standpoint of the child, the great waste in the school comes from his inability to utilize the experiences he gets outside the school in any complete and free way within the school itself; while on the other hand, he is unable to apply in daily life what he is learning in school. That is the isolation of the school—its isolation from life.

(Dewey, 1916)

C hapter 3 deals with the research that supports authentic learning, how to plan and develop authentic learning activities, and how to assess authentic learning; finally, it explores several examples of authentic learning activities in various content areas. It's important to understand that unless students possess at least a rudimentary *conceptual* understanding of the phenomenon they are investigating, the authentic learning activity may lead to little or no gain in their relevant knowledge and may be little more than busy work (Kirschner, Sweller, & Clark, 2006; Mayer, 2004). Authentic learning involving serious inquiry will not necessarily ensure meaningful learning unless we make certain students are prepared to learn from it.

The Link Between Preparation and Meaning

In the Diesel Engine Operation and Tune-up Course, taught in the Heavy Equipment Technology Program at Ferris State University, students are required each semester to solve a real-world industry problem. The students

focus on an issue that they discovered from course discussions with the professor, through interacting with guest speakers, or during field trips to companies in the industry. The problem is usually related to maintenance
practices, engine diagnosis, use of new fuels, or other instructor-approved
industry concerns that students bring forward. The students work in teams
to solve the problem and prepare a 30-minute presentation that explains
their problem-solving process and solution(s). The students also receive
training in how to make a professional presentation and give input to the
rubric that is used to evaluate their presentations. The presentation is made
to members of the heavy equipment industry. Because I provide the professional presentation training and have assisted the instructor in refining the
rubric, I have witnessed firsthand the dynamics of this authentic learning
experience. This course activity not only affords students a real-world learning experience but also provides a networking opportunity with industry
professionals that can lead to internships and employment. This is authentic
learning at its best.

A Definition

"Authentic learning is a pedagogical approach that allows students to
explore, discuss, and meaningfully construct concepts and relationships in
contexts that involve real-world problems and projects that are relevant to
the learner" (Donovan, Bransford, & Pellegrino, 1999). It embodies not only
the use of real problems and issues but seeks to have students use methods
that are used in the real world, including teamwork and collaboration, technology, and the professional presentation of processes and solutions. The use
of authentic learning experiences increases students' motivation because it
involves active engagement and meaningful outcomes that others (industry
professionals in the case of the heavy-equipment students) actually want and
need.

Authentic learning is hardly a new concept. It was the primary mode of
instruction for apprentices who, after learning in the real world, would take
their place as one of the trained craftspeople of their day. However, as the
numbers of students rose in the 19th century, it became difficult to manage
not only the increased number of students but also the increased amount of
liability issues at the worksites. These combinations put severe limits on the
apprenticeship process (Harrington, Oliver, & Reeves, 2003). Soon, other
ways of education were developed that often moved students away from real-
world experiences.

Many in education have argued that all would-be scientists, mathematicians, engineers, and historians need to be "enculturated" into the discipline—and the earlier, the better (Lave & Wenger, 1991). Along with memorizing facts and practicing technical procedures, beginning students should be learning what John Seely Brown calls the "genres" of the discipline. This is the schema through which full members of the disciplinary community "recognize whether a problem is an important problem, or a solution an elegant solution, or even what constitutes a solution in the first place" (J. S. Brown, 1999). What's more, students should know what it feels like for actual stakeholders beyond the classroom to hold them accountable for their work products. Whether the learning activity results in a business plan, a set of design specifications, a presentation to the city council, or a short film, authentic evaluation occurs naturally over the course of the project, and the authentic evaluation comes from several sources, just as it would in real life, including peers, supervisors, and clients. The goal is to give learners the confidence that comes with being recognized as "legitimate peripheral participants" in a community of practice (Lombardi, 2007).

As our students look to their futures, they need to recognize that the attributes that will separate those with career-transcending prospects from those who have little opportunity for advancement are expert thinking and complex communication skills (Levy & Murnane, 2005). Expert thinking involves the ability to identify and solve problems for which there is no routine solution. This requires pattern recognition and metacognition. Another differentiator is complex communication, such as persuading, explaining, negotiating, gaining trust, and building understanding. Although foundational skills such as reading, writing, mathematics, history, and language remain essential, a more complex set of competencies is required today (Levy & Murnane, 2005). For employers, the most important skills in new hires include teamwork, critical thinking/reasoning, assembling/organizing information, and innovative thinking/creativity (Hart, 2006). Authentic learning activities help develop these very skills.

Research Support for Authentic Learning

You do not need to be a brain scientist to recognize that students come alive when the learning is dynamic, significant, and relevant to their lives. However, brain scientists have demonstrated why students react so favorably to authentic learning experiences. As mentioned in chapter 1, this favorable reaction occurs because learning activates the reward pathway in the brain. This reinforcement pathway is composed of both central nervous system structures and endogenous neurotransmitters communicating between these structures. The reward pathway evolved to promote activities that are essential to the survival of the human race as well as other mammals (Lowinson, Ruiz, Millman, & Langrod, 1997). When we get hungry and seek out nourishment (and I don't mean a double cheeseburger) to satisfy our hunger, our brain releases neurochemicals (specifically dopamine) that make us feel good so we will want to satisfy our hunger in the future and stay alive. As mentioned in chapter 1, cognitive neuroscientist Dr. Janet Zadina explained that the reward pathway is stimulated in students when learning is active, meaningful, and authentic (Zadina, 2010). According to the Genetics Science Learning Center (GSLC) website at the University of Utah (http://learn.gen etics.utah.edu/) the brain ensures that we repeat these survival behaviors whenever possible by connecting the parts that control memory and behavior (Genetics Science Learning Center, 2010). When students engage in authentic learning experiences in which they have recognized the relevance of the experience either on their own or through our assistance, they feel rewarded and they want to keep getting that feeling.

A note to keep in mind comes from the research of psychologist Kelly Lambert. Dr. Lambert's findings have shown that results that come too easily can actually have a negative emotional impact. Lambert hypothesized that rigor is part of the reward pathway. Throughout most of the history of humanity, survival was rigorous. Getting and preparing food, for example, required enormous effort. Therefore, there was a subsequent feeling of pleasure and gratification from the results of this effort. The task for teachers is to make the learning experience both meaningful and challenging.

In the 1950s, Jean Piaget was already advocating that schools must get learners actively engaged in real-world learning (Piaget, 1954). Since then, constructivists have shown that learning becomes active when students can connect new knowledge with their prior knowledge and a meaningful context (Brown, Collins, & Duguid, 1989). For all teachers, bringing the real world into the classroom is key to promoting students' learning.

Traditional learning situations, in which students are passive recipients of knowledge, are inconsistent with the learning circumstances of real life (Lave, 1988). Teaching in which there is an absence of meaning breeds low engagement and inhibits learning transfer (Newmann, Secada, & Wehlage, 1995). Harvard psychologist and multiple intelligences theorist Howard Gardner said that school for many has become nothing more than drill and response; there is no relevance for the material the students are expected to learn (Gardner, 1999). This view was reinforced by findings from major studies of U.S. high schools over the past decade that find the schools mostly unchanged from how they operated 40 years ago, despite significant increases in dollars, technology, and research on learning (U.S. Department of Education, National Commission on The High School Senior Year, 2001). I am not trying to pass judgment on U.S. high schools; they face very different problems than we in higher education face in the classroom. I am pointing out that the teacher-centered learning experiences our students had in high school have left them hungry for more active and authentic learning, and higher education has the ability to provide it if we embrace a learner-centered path.

Features of Authentic Learning

Various versions of authentic learning features exist; they were created as guides to help teachers design authentic learning experiences. I have used one set of these features in the following list as a means of demonstrating how they relate to an authentic learning experience. I used the writing of this book as an example of their application.

Authentic learning, as described by the North Central Regional Educational Laboratory, does the following:

1. Deals with a real-world task. I am writing this book to make a difference in how teaching happens in higher education, which I see as an important real-world task.
2. Has value beyond a school setting. If this book were an academic assignment, I would learn some valuable information about writing, editing, and research. Because I know that this book will affect both teachers and their students in a valuable way, the work of writing it is more meaningful and worthwhile to me.
3. Is interdisciplinary. I am using information from neuroscience, biology, cognitive science, psychology, evolutionary biology, and other fields, and I am developing language skills, as I make my case for a learner-centered practice.
4. Allows a variety of learning styles. I am free to use any approach I want to produce the best product.

5. Affords students the opportunity to take ownership of their learning. I am heavily invested in this project and see it as having great importance to me. I know that I have control over what goes into this book. I also see it as a meaningful use of my time and talents.

6. Is student driven. As the one writing this book, I am the student working to complete a meaningful assignment I have chosen for myself. I am exploring research to share with you, and I am relating personal experiences that can make learner-centered teaching successful.

7. Positions the teacher as a facilitator. My own knowledge is only one of the many resources I used in this book. While I have had some input from facilitators of knowledge pertaining to this subject, this is not a teacher-centered activity.

8. Uses scaffolding to assist learning. I regularly turn to research and to colleagues for help whenever I need it. It will be a better book because of their help, but I also feel a strong sense of personal accomplishment that belongs just to me. This is the exact way I try to use scaffolding in my teaching. I want the students to be successful so I help when they need it, but I know it's vital that they experience a personal sense of accomplishment.

9. Uses real-time data that students may investigate and draw conclusions from. What I am writing reflects up-to-date research findings about human learning and the teaching process. I use my critical thinking and advanced comprehension skills to relate meaning from separate resources.

10. Encourages students to work together and discuss how to solve problems. I regularly talk with colleagues about my ideas for this book and discuss their opinions and advice on how to present certain ideas in the best way possible.

11. Asks students to produce a product that is directed toward a real audience. You are reading this book. I have been successful in reaching this outcome.

An authentic learning experience does not need to have all of these features to be worthwhile. The goal is to use these features to guide the development of learning activities that are more authentic in nature. Figure 3.1 identifies an additional set of characteristics for authentic learning tasks that can aid us in designing these authentic activities.

FIGURE 3.1
Traits of Authentic Education

1. Authentic activities have real-world relevance.
2. Authentic activities are ill-defined, requiring students to define the tasks and sub-tasks needed to complete the activity.
3. Authentic activities comprise complex tasks to be investigated by students over a sustained period of time.
4. Authentic activities provide the opportunity for students to examine the task from different perspectives, using a variety of resources.
5. Authentic activities provide the opportunity to collaborate.
6. Authentic activities provide the opportunity to reflect.
7. Authentic activities can be integrated and applied across different subject areas and lead beyond domain specific outcomes.
8. Authentic activities are seamlessly integrated with assessment.
9. Authentic activities create polished products valuable in their own right rather than as preparation for something else.
10. Authentic activities allow competing solutions and diversity of outcome.

Source: Herrington, Oliver, & Reeves (2003).

Designing an Authentic Experience

In a 2006 content analysis of 45 articles describing authentic learning in different disciplines, four themes emerged supporting the design of authentic learning: (1) The activity involves real-world problems that mimic the work of professionals in the discipline, with presentation of findings to audiences beyond the classroom; (2) open-ended inquiry, thinking skills, and metacognition are addressed; (3) students engage in discourse and social learning in a community of learners; and (4) students are empowered through choice to direct their own learning in relevant project work (Rule, 2006).

In her Educause White Paper, "Approaches That Work: How Authentic Learning Is Transforming Higher Education," Marilyn M. Lombardi offered similar suggestions for those of us seeking to create more meaningful learning experiences in our classrooms:

- Instructors are encouraged to design activities for their students that are as similar as possible to the real-world tasks of industry professionals.
- The challenges that students are asked to undertake should be complex, ambiguous, and multifaceted in nature, thus requiring sustained investigation.

- Reflection, self-assessment, and performance review are fully integrated into the exercise. The real-world challenge comes with its own criteria for success. Students are held accountable based on their skill levels, maturity, and task readiness for achieving the milestones that practitioners would have to meet under genuine working conditions.
- Teamwork is as essential to the authentic learning experience as it would be in modern workplace settings. Groups of students have to draw on multiple sources and negotiate among multiple perspectives, including those of the stakeholders (business partners, clients, customers, citizens) who will be affected by their performance (Lombardi, 2007).

An authentic learning activity is designed to draw on the existing talents and experiences of students, building their confidence through participation and helping them see the connection between personal aptitude and professional practice. The activity is matched to the needs of the new participatory learner, one whose expectations for active, hands-on involvement in learning have been raised by the proliferation of creative opportunities, now available through a multitude of media tools (Lombardi, 2007).

Examples of Authentic Learning Experiences in Higher Education Classrooms

Indeed, it can be argued that when students see that complex theory has real-life application, it is no longer "uni work," becoming instead knowledge and understandings that have clear value to their professional lives. (Ferry, Kervin, Carrington, & Prcevich, 2007)

It is important to remember that authenticity does not mean you have to take students to the Louvre to learn about art, but rather that we work to increase the amount of authenticity involved in the learning tasks we give our students. For example, tasks can fall on a continuum of authenticity where memorizing facts about paintings would be less authentic than visiting a website that has a guided tour. But the guided tour is less authentic than actually visiting the museum. Faculty members should aim to make students' experiences as similar as possible to what happens in real life and, in doing so, should provide support for the students to be reflective and to learn (Marra, 2010).

The following are examples taken from higher education institutions and design companies around the world that demonstrate how we could all enhance the authentic learning of our students. By borrowing from our colleagues or purchasing activities that can be adapted to the classroom, we can bring more authentic learning experiences to our students.

Palestine—The Game. This game, developed by Serious Games Interactive, allows students to take the role of a journalist experiencing the Israeli–Palestinian conflict.

Virtual Courtroom. Harvard University presents a course in cyberspace on the creation and delivery of persuasive arguments for courts of law.

Astronomical Milestones Exhibits. In the University of Arizona's astronomy class, students research, build, and script exhibits for milestones in the Earth's 4.6-billion-year history.

Sim Port—The Game. The objective of the game Sim Port, developed by Tygron, is to assist Port of Rotterdam employees, both individually and collectively, in making appropriate planning and implementation decisions for creating a workable design for reclaiming the next lot of land from the North Sea over a 30-year period.

Visible Human Project. The Visible Human Project (VHP) uses the resources of the National Institutes of Health, National Library of Medicine (NLM) to enhance significantly the teaching of anatomy and physiology by giving students access to realistic visuals of the human body. VHP is an outgrowth of the NLM's 1986 long-range plan. It contains complete, anatomically detailed, three-dimensional representations of normal male and female human bodies. The VHP has generated 18,000 digitized sections of the human body. The long-term goal is to produce a system of knowledge structures that will transparently link visual knowledge forms to symbolic knowledge formats (National Library of Medicine, 2010). This massive website allows students to learn a great deal on their own: It includes guided tours through the human body while also providing teachers visual resources to supplement coursework, making the learning much more genuine.

Borderlands Issue Project. At the University of Texas at El Paso, preservice educators enrolled in a social studies methods course work with middle school students from a local public magnet school to co-plan, co-design, and co-present issue-centered projects concerning the local

U.S.-Mexico border. The goals are to develop well-reasoned responses based on disciplined inquiry and in-depth study, and to move beyond relativistic notions of truth. The teams co-presented their projects during the local school's Parent Night. This authentic experience helped middle school students to learn collaboration skills needed to co-plan, co-research, co-design, and co-teach complex issues with others; the preservice educators discovered that the middle school students exceeded performance expectations (Cashman, 2007). This issue-centered project model is easy to adapt to almost any course or student group.

Educational Statistics Course Community Collaboration. At the University of West Florida, a community outreach research and authentic learning (CORAL) center connects educational statistics faculty members and students with community agencies and organizations that need real-world, data-driven research. Community Action Projects for Students Utilizing Leadership and E-based Statistics (CAPSULES) engage graduate students in service-learning projects of managing, conducting, and delivering authentic data-driven research. The graduate educational program includes: (1) statistics courses with real-world active learning and authentic assessment; (2) opportunities for graduate students to engage in team-driven quantitative research prior to the thesis or dissertation experience with community agency/educational institution–generated projects; and (3) community action projects in which graduate students can serve as research managers, leaders, and presenters (Thompson, 2009).

Model Eliciting Activities

Model eliciting activities (MEAs) were developed by mathematics education researchers (Lesh, 1998) to better understand and encourage problem solving. An MEA is an activity that is "thought-revealing and model-eliciting" (Lesh et al., 2000) and has been adapted for other areas such as engineering (Diefes-Dux et al., 2004) and gifted education (Chamberain & Moon, 2005). MEAs are designed to encourage students to build mathematical models in order to solve complex problems, as well as provide a means for educators to better understand students' thinking. MEAs are based on six specific principles, and they involve careful development and field testing.

1. *Model construction principle:* Problems must be designed to allow for the creation of a model dealing with elements, relationships, and

operations among the elements, and patterns and rules governing such relationships.

2. *Reality principle:* Problems must be meaningful and relevant to the students.
3. *Self-assessment principle:* Students must be able to self-assess and measure the usefulness of their solutions.
4. *Construct documentation principle:* Students must be able to reveal and document their thinking processes within their solution.
5. *Construct shareability and reusability principle:* Solutions created by students should be generalizable or easily adapted to other situations.
6. *Effective prototype principle:* Others should be able to interpret solutions easily (Lesh et al., 2000).

Examples of MEAs

The complete lesson plans for the following examples can be found on the Carleton University website at http://serc.carleton.edu/sp/search/index.html.

Judging Airlines. Students examine data on departure delays for five airlines flying out of Chicago's O'Hare Airport. The task is to develop a model to determine which airline has the best chance of departing on time. Students write a report that identifies the best airline and the reasoning behind their decision.

Identifying a Theft Suspect. This MEA challenges students to develop a model for predicting the characteristics of a person who has committed a crime. Students work with real data on shoe length, height, and gender to develop the model. Students write a report to the crime victim that identifies a suspect and justifies their decision for choosing that person. The activity sets the stage for students to learn about regression models and reinforces their understanding of central tendency and variability. It is suggested that this activity be used prior to a formal introduction to linear relationships.

Creating a Spam Filter. This activity asks students to work in a team to develop a set of rules that can be used to program a spam filter for a client. Students are given samples of spam and nonspam subject lines to examine. The rules they develop are based on characteristics of the subject lines of e-mails. After the rules are ready, students are given a test set of data to use and are asked to come up with a numerical measure to quantify how well their method (model) works. Each team writes a report describing how its model works and how well it performed on the test data. This activity can serve as an introduction to ideas of classification. The activity can also be the basis for introducing students to types of statistical errors.

Use of Standards in Creating Authentic Learning Activities

One effective way to engage our students in authentic learning activities is to use established professional standards from various academic areas as guidelines in developing learning tasks. I have included one example that shows how this process can work.

Standards for Instrumental Arranging

The following standards were developed by Hank Vaughn and posted on Jon Mueller's Authentic Assessment Toolbox website (http://jfmueller.facul ty.noctrl.edu/toolbox/). From these standards, instrumental music teachers can develop authentic tasks that have students working to meet the professional standards of the music field. In this example of standards, students will be able to

- Create an original instrumental arrangement using at least five voices.
- Demonstrate appropriate voicing for instrumental arrangements.
- Conduct the ensemble.
- Score arrangements with proper instrumental range.
- Rehearse the ensemble through their arrangement.
- Rearrange musical arrangements to fit their instrumentation.
- Create different timbres within their arrangements.

Composition and Authentic Learning

One of the basic principles of a learner-centered practice is that students learn to take on more responsibility for their work. The reason for this is simple: They will be responsible for their own work the rest of their lives. So what better way to enhance the focus and effort of writing assignments than to have the pieces read by authentic audiences? The following are some examples:

1. Encourage students to write a letter to the editor of their hometown newspapers or the local paper where they are attending school. The

letter could address a real-world issue they care about or a topic area where they would like to see a change take place.

2. Have students write essays on current news topics that interest them. Then guide the students in submitting the essays to their local, home, or college newspaper so that their essays can perhaps be published.

3. Post students' course writing assignments on a class website where all members of the class can read them. This public posting also allows for peer review. You can assign a team of students to read a few of their peers' writings and, using a rubric, give the student writers constructive feedback.

4. Request students to write a plausible solution to a real problem on their campus and have them submit their solutions to the appropriate campus office.

5. Publish a class magazine or book of writings and distribute it around campus.

6. Use the calibrated peer review (CPR) system. This is a free, web-based program (http://www.educause.edu/ir/library/pdf/ELI5002 .pdf) that allows instructors to incorporate frequent writing assignments into their courses, regardless of class size, without increasing their grading workload. Students are trained to be competent reviewers and are then given the responsibility of providing their classmates with personalized feedback on expository writing assignments. Meanwhile, with access to all student work, instructors can monitor the class as a whole and assess the progress of each student. The CPR system manages the entire peer-review process, including assignment creation, electronic paper submission, student training in reviewing, student input analysis, and final performance report preparation.

The key element is to let students' work receive as much authentic review as possible because that is how their work will be judged when they leave campus.

Why Use Authentic Assessment Tools?

What you assess is what you get; if you don't test it you won't get it. (Resnick, 1987)

There are many definitions of authentic assessment, but most share very similar views of what we seek to accomplish by using these tools. According to the American Library Association, authentic assessment is an evaluation process that involves multiple forms of performance measurement, reflecting the student's learning, achievement, motivation, and attitudes on instructionally relevant activities. Examples of authentic assessment techniques include performance assessment, portfolios, and self-assessment. The New Horizons for Learning (NHL) educational website defines authentic assessment as evaluating by asking for the behavior the learning is intended to produce. The concept of model, practice, and feedback in which students learn what excellent performance is and are guided to practice an entire concept rather than bits and pieces in preparation for eventual understanding is the key to authentic assessment (Keller,2011). Traditional assessment, by contrast, relies on indirect or proxy items: efficient, simplistic substitutes from which we think valid inferences can be made about students' performance (Wiggens, 1990). To improve students' performance, we must recognize that essential intellectual abilities are falling through the cracks of conventional testing (Wiggens, 1990). If we are to ensure that our students receive the optimal level of preparation to face the many possible futures that await them, we need to measure their learning using the very tools that learning will be measured against when they leave our institutions. When I first started presenting on the topic of learner-centered teaching 15 years ago, I used the slide presented in Figure 3.2 to make this very point.

FIGURE 3.2
What Employers Want

Colleges and universities work very hard to define the skills and knowledge they want their graduates to have, but unfortunately they use traditional assessment tools that often don't measure whether the learning has occurred. For example, every college and university claims they want their graduates to have excellent speaking and listening skills, but they give mostly multiple-choice or other forms of written tests that don't give any indication whether these skills are being developed. If we really want our students to have these communication skills, then we need to create authentic activities where the skills are used and assess them based on real-world expectations so the feedback can help the students to improve.

Grant Wiggens, in his 1990 article "The Case for Authentic Assessment," outlined reasons why authentic assessment techniques are much better than traditional assessment techniques in measuring student learning:

1. Authentic assessments require students to be effective performers with acquired knowledge. Traditional tests tend to reveal only whether the students can recognize, recall, or "plug in" what was learned out of context. This may be as problematic as inferring that a student is a good driver from a written test alone.

2. Authentic assessments present students with the full array of tasks that mirror the priorities and challenges found in the best instructional activities: conducting research; writing, revising, and discussing papers; providing an engaging oral analysis of a recent political event; collaborating with others in a debate; etc.

3. Authentic assessments attend to whether students can craft polished, thorough, and justifiable answers, performances, or products. Conventional tests typically ask students only to select or write correct responses, without assessing their reasoning processes.

4. Authentic assessment achieves validity and reliability by emphasizing and standardizing the appropriate criteria for scoring varied products; traditional testing standardizes objective items and, hence, the (one) right answer for each. "Test validity" should depend in part upon whether the test simulates real-world *tests* of ability.

5. Authentic tasks involve loosely structured challenges and roles that help students rehearse for the complex ambiguities in adult and professional life. Traditional tests are more like drills, assessing static and arbitrarily discrete or simplistic elements of those activities. We rehearse for and teach with authentic tests in mind (think of music and military training) without compromising validity.

6. In many colleges and all professional settings, the essential challenges are known in advance: the upcoming report, recital, board presentation, legal case, book to write, etc. Traditional tests, by requiring complete secrecy for their validity, make it difficult for teachers and students to rehearse and gain the confidence that comes from knowing their performance obligations. A known challenge also makes it possible to hold all students to higher standards.

7. Authentic assessment also has the advantage of providing parents and community members with directly observable products and understandable evidence concerning their students' performance; the quality of student work is more discernible to laypersons than when we must rely on translations of talk about stanines and renorming (Wiggens, 1990).

By advocating for authentic assessment as a means of improving student learning, I am not suggesting that testing for knowledge that is vital to the performance of authentic tasks does not have a place in higher education. If student do not know the language of a subject, it is very difficult to have them make a presentation or write a letter to the editor.

Students want to see that how and what they are being asked to learn is relevant and meaningful to their lives. Using authentic assessments that challenge students to reach real-world standards clearly shows them the relevance of the learning. See Figure 3.3 for examples of authentic assessment.

Use of Rubrics

One effective tool for evaluating authentic learning activities is a rubric designed to reflect the standards of the profession or industry that the students are preparing to enter. Most professions and industries have published lists of standards that can be use to create meaningful rubrics. The Internet is full of excellent sources for rubric construction and literally thousands of ready-to-use rubrics in almost every content area. Figure 3.4 is an example of a rubric that can be used to measure the level of collaboration taking place in teams that are working to solve an authentic problem.

E-Portfolio as Proof of Learning

The University of Texas at Austin, College of Engineering introduced Polaris, an in-house e-portfolio system made available to all engineering

FIGURE 3.3
Examples of Authentic Assessment

- Measurement taking
- Oral report
- Written report
- Debate
- Portfolio
- Lab report
- Science notebook/journal
- Student talk
- Active listening
- Concept map
- Open-ended questions
- Lab performance
- Interview
- Skills/Behaviors check list
- Self-evaluation
- Peer evaluation
- Outside professional evaluation
- Use of industry standards
- Product production—objects, movies, art forms, scripts, advertisements, etc.
- Public presentation at professional meetings, conferences

Source: jove.geol.niu.edu/faculty/kitts/GEOL401/inquiryassessment401.ppt

students. Polaris was produced by the college's Faculty Innovation Center (FIC), in collaboration with the mechanical engineering department and with support from Ford Motor Company. The portfolio system is not just for résumés and other documents; the Polaris framework includes special exercises designed to help engineering students reflect on the relevance of their course projects and experiences as a means to better understand their development as engineers. Prompts and exercises assist students in describing their projects accurately, in terms that dovetail with those established by the Accreditation Board for Engineering and Technology (ABET). The unique element of this system is that it guides students through the description and analysis of their own coursework. The system uses a metacognitive strategy that encourages students to study their own learning patterns in an effort to improve their performance over time (EDUCAUSE Learning Initiative, 2006).

FIGURE 3.4
Collaborative Work Skills

Category	4	3	2	1
Working With Others	Almost always listens to, shares with, and supports the efforts of others. Tries to keep people working well together.	Usually listens to, shares, with, and supports the efforts of others. Does not cause "waves" in the group.	Often listens to, shares with, and supports the efforts of others, but sometimes is not a good team member.	Rarely listens to, shares with, and supports the efforts of others. Often is not a good team player.
Task Focus	Consistently stays focused on the task and what needs to be done. Very self-directed.	Focuses on the task and what needs to be done most of the time. Other group members can count on this person.	Focuses on the task and what needs to be done some of the time. Other group members must sometimes nag, prod, and remind to keep this person on-task.	Rarely focuses on the task and what needs to be done. Lets others do the work.
Quality of Work	Provides work of the highest quality.	Provides high-quality work.	Provides work that occasionally needs to be checked/redone by other group members to ensure quality.	Provides work that usually needs to be checked/redone by others to ensure quality.
Effort	Work reflects this student's best efforts.	Work reflects a strong effort from this student.	Work reflects some effort from this student.	Work reflects very little effort on the part of this student.
Attitude	Never is publicly critical of the project or the work of others. Always has a positive attitude about the task(s).	Rarely is publicly critical of the project or the work of others. Often has a positive attitude about the task(s).	Occasionally is publicly critical of the project or the work of other members of the group. Usually has a positive attitude about the task(s).	Often is publicly critical of the project or the work of other members of the group. Often has a negative attitude about the task(s).
Contributions	Routinely provides useful ideas. A definite leader who contributes a lot of effort.	Usually provides useful ideas. A strong group member who tries hard!	Sometimes provides useful ideas. A satisfactory group member who does what is required.	Rarely provides useful ideas. May refuse to participate.
Time Management	Routinely uses time well throughout the project to ensure things get done on time. Group does not have to adjust deadlines or work responsibilities.	Usually uses time well throughout the project. Group does not have to adjust deadlines or work responsibilities.	Tends to procrastinate, but always gets things done by the deadlines. Group does not have to adjust deadlines or work responsibilities.	Rarely gets things done by the deadlines and group has to adjust deadlines or work responsibilities because of this person's inadequate time management.

Authentic Learning: You Can Do This

Integrating authentic learning experiences and assessments into your daily teaching requires only that you decide to do so. The planning needed to create lessons that are authentic requires no more time or effort than planning traditional lessons. We need only to decide that we want our students, as John Muller, one of the leading voices in the field of authentic learning, says, not just to know history, math, or science but to do history, math, and science, and then we must plan accordingly.

4

FROM LECTURER
TO FACILITATOR

The greatest sign of success for a teacher . . . is
to be able to say, "The students are now working
as if I did not exist."

(Maria Montessori, 1949)

I t is 20 minutes before his next class. He walks into his office, opens a
file drawer, pulls out a set of lecture notes on today's topic, and walks
down the hall to class. He arrives early; greets the students waiting for
class to begin; and, exactly at noon, begins talking about life in 16th-century
France, how to recognize certain plants in the woods of northern Michigan,
or about any of a thousand other topics. Those students actually in attendance take some notes and try to stay awake, listening for any clues about
the upcoming test. A few students ask questions, but that is the extent of the
interaction between the teacher and the students. The information given is
accurate and up-to-date, and parts of it are even interesting to some students.
The clock ticks on for 50, 75, or 180 minutes until class comes to an end.
No assignment is given and the students leave, talking about lunch.

This scenario plays out in thousands of higher education classrooms
across the nation every day. It is not that the teacher in the scenario is
unprepared or unconcerned about student learning or that his expertise is
not up-to-date; it is simply that he missed out on an opportunity to optimize
his students' learning because much of what went on in the classroom
required him to fire his own neuron networks rather than requiring the
students to build their own new networks or fire networks of prior knowledge. The difference between a traditional, lecture-based instructional model
and learner-centered teaching (LCT) lies in whose neuron networks get fired
and wired.

To view chapter-related videos please go to tinyurl.com/learnercenteredvideo.

The Power of Planning

It is not a simple task to move away from a traditional, lecture-centered model of instruction. It requires learning new skills and spending more time in planning each class. It requires locating resources that students can investigate on their own or in groups. It also requires new forms of assessment, both formative and summative. However, it results in most of the neuron firing and wiring occurring in the students' brains, and that is exactly what we want their brains to be doing. This chapter offers a plan on how to move from a teller of information to a facilitator of learning. The plan is not complicated to follow, but it does require more time, planning, and effort than just reaching for a set of lecture notes.

What Is a Facilitator?

We hear the term *facilitator* used all the time in numerous professional and educational contexts. In business and industry, the term often refers to a person who runs meetings, oversees committees, or gets others to complete a task or reach a goal. In education, it most often means supporting students in learning their course material by providing an environment for engagement; a set of resources such as questions, articles, research findings, problems, and/or cases to engage with; and using assessment tools that provide the learner with meaningful feedback.

If you take a few minutes to search the Internet using the terms *facilitator, effective facilitation,* and/or *facilitating learning,* the suggested sites have one commonality: They offer specific instructions on becoming an effective facilitator in specific content areas. The sites do not assume that you were born to facilitate or that you know how to facilitate the learning of a group of people. They all acknowledge that facilitation is a learned skill.

A Definition

The idea that educators are facilitators of learning and change has been around for at least half a century. It was the work of Carl Rogers in the United States and Josephine Klein in Britain in the early 1960s that brought the idea to the fore (Smith, 2001). Many of us have been trying to facilitate some aspects of our students' learning ever since we first heard the term *active learning.* Unfortunately, our efforts, rather than being encouraged, were often met with pressure from administrators or colleagues to maintain the traditional lecture approach (a pressure I still hear faculty members speak about even today) or research demands, which make it difficult to find the time to plan more learning activities. Or sometimes we simply felt uncomfortable with the role of being a facilitator.

The facilitator's job is to support everyone in doing his or her best thinking and practice. To do this, the facilitator encourages full participation, promotes mutual understanding, and cultivates shared responsibility. By supporting everyone to do their best thinking, the facilitator enables group members to search for inclusive solutions and build sustainable agreements (Kaner et al., 2007).

Effective facilitation also involves thorough knowledge about the particular topic or content that the group is addressing. This role of teacher as expert does not change when moving from a teller of knowledge to a facilitator of learning. What changes is how this expertise is used. The discussion of scaffolding in chapter 2 is one example of this.

The Plan

Step One: Writing Daily Learning Outcomes

I began my educational career teaching Grades 3 through 6. Although I lasted only a very short time as an elementary teacher, I did learn the value of preparing lesson plans. I have carried this practice to my college teaching, and it has served me well for the past 34 years, especially when I moved to an LCT approach. My lesson planning always begins with learning outcomes. Defining what we want our students to know or be able to do as a result of engaging in 50, 75, or 180 minutes of course activity is the first step toward effective teaching, whether you are a teller or a facilitator. You cannot know if your time and efforts were well spent if you don't know what you wanted the students to learn. As my son often says to me on the golf practice range, when I ask him if he thought my shot was good, "That depends. Where were you aiming?"

Most of us teaching in higher education today have learning outcomes in our syllabi. To be a learner-centered facilitator, however, you need to have daily outcomes that drive the planning process. A learning outcome involves four simple but important questions:

1. Who will be doing the learning?
2. When will the learning be completed?

3. What will the students be able to do or know?
4. How will you know they learned it?

It is especially vital that questions 3 and 4 have clearly defined answers. For example, a learning outcome for my reading course for the second day of class is, "Students will, by the end of class, demonstrate their ability to annotate college textbook material by annotating two pages from a psychology textbook and submitting it for teacher review."

By taking the time to define my learning outcomes for each class, I am in a position to indentify several important questions that need to be answered to make the class successful and to ensure that I act as a facilitator of my students' learning. The following are questions that you should ask yourself when defining your learning outcomes:

1. What is the best use of my time during class to help students reach this outcome?
2. What will my students do both in and out of class to reach this outcome?
3. What resources will I need to provide my students so they can accomplish this learning?
4. What resources will my students need to provide themselves so they can accomplish this learning?
5. How much time do I need to allocate to the various parts of the instruction, practice, and feedback of this lesson?
6. Will the students work alone, in pairs, or in groups?
7. How will I assess this learning?

These questions represent the outline of my lesson plan. The answers to each question give me my action plan.

Step Two: Action Plan

Because my learning outcome is to have students learn how to annotate college text material, my actions, which are the answers to the seven questions (repeated in abbreviated form), are as follows:

1. *What is the best use of my time?* My time is best used explaining why annotation is such an important reading skill. I will demonstrate how to annotate text and answer any questions students have about how to annotate a college text.

2. *What will students do?* My students will be expected to listen and take appropriate notes from the explanation and demonstration on annotation. They will then work on applying what they have learned to two pages of college-level text. Finally, they will be asked to present to the class (using the document camera) a few examples of their annotations. Finally, they will hand in their annotations for my review and feedback.

3. *What resources will I need?* I will need a sample handout of a completed annotation of college text that students can use as a model and a handout of two pages of college text that students will annotate in class. I will need a few PowerPoint slides providing images of annotation to use during my explanation. I will also need to have a page of college text that I can annotate as demonstration using the document camera.

4. *What resources will students need?* Students will need a writing utensil and notebook paper.

5. *Allocation of class time?* In a 75-minute class period, I will need 15 minutes for my explanatory presentation. Students will use 45 minutes to annotate text. Then there will be 10 minutes for annotation presentations. The last 5 minutes are for wrap-up. (*Note:* Because I have taught reading for many years, I am familiar with how long my explanation and demonstration will take. If you are new to teaching or teaching a lesson for the first time, you can only make a best guess and adapt as needed when estimating time.)

6. *Will the students work alone or in pairs?* In this case, students will be working alone because I want to assess their individual annotation skills.

7. *How will I assess the learning?* I will have two pages of text from each student to review, which will allow me to determine what they have learned. I will be grading each paper according to the following criteria questions: (a) Did the student identify the key information? (b) Did the student use his or her own words? (c) Did the student identify the terms and definitions? (d) Did the student use abbreviations correctly?

I realize that many teachers often do similar steps in their head. However, taking the time to think through each question and make lesson plan notes will ensure that you have made every effort not only to optimize your students' learning (the heart of an LCT practice), but to move from your role of a teller to that of a facilitator.

Step Three: Additional Practice

The next step in planning a facilitation of learning is to decide on the additional activities and practice students need to further their understanding of the new knowledge or improve their use of a new skill. We all know this step as "homework." In a learner-centered model, this step is crucial to our goals of promoting long-term learning and engaging students in authentic and meaningful practice. The activities students engage in outside class are just as important as the activities in class. Consider the following when developing learning experiences to be completed outside the class period:

1. What additional help do students need to better understand the new material or become more proficient in the skill?
2. What is the best way to deliver this help?
3. What resources do students need to continue their learning?
4. Do students need feedback on what they did in class before trying additional activities?

These questions can help us decide what homework assignments are most effective and keep out-of-class learning from becoming busy work. I address these questions to any homework I assign. The following are examples of how I would answer the questions (some repeated in abbreviated form) for the lesson on annotation:

1. *What additional help do students need?* Knowing that annotation is the most important comprehension and recall skill we teach in our reading course, I know that students need a great deal of practice to master it. I will not be assigning any annotation homework until I have given my students feedback on their in-class annotations. I don't want my students practicing bad habits, and I want them to understand what effective annotation looks like. Then I will assign out-of-class practice on a regular basis. In your course, it is integral to decide how important each new chunk of information or new skill is to the outcomes of the course. This allows you to decide how much additional practice is needed to help students reach their learning goal.
2. *What is the best way to deliver this help?* My students have a course textbook full of chapters reprinted from other college textbooks, and I regularly ask them to work on material from these chapters. With the enormous amount of resources available online, excellent practice

materials can be found in a thoughtful perusal of sites. The major advantage in using the Internet is the almost limitless amount of practice that can be provided if we develop activities and store them electronically. Feedback can also be given electronically, either by the software program being used or by the instructor. For example, providing students with a large pool of practice questions or problems where they receive instant feedback on their accuracy has been shown to improve learning and recall (Rawson, 2010).

3. *What resources do students need?* In my course, students need only their course textbook; however, it is likely that students will need additional materials in your course. Resources for course practice are crucial to providing an effective learning experience. Practice of authentic work over time is a pillar of LCT. There is no doubt that a lot of time and work will go into providing practice materials that support course understanding and skill development. This kind of development is one of the real differences between LCT and a traditional classroom experience where students might read the textbook outside class and study for a test every four weeks.

4. *Do students need feedback before practicing?* In the specific case of my reading class, I believe they do. I don't want students repeating the same errors they may have made in class doing work outside class. However, this is a question that each of us must answer individually for each teaching situation. I pose the question here because the specific issue of practicing bad habits was a point that was stressed when I was working with our dental hygiene faculty members. They do not allow students to practice their instrument skills at home because they have found that the skills are so intricate and subtle that it is easy for students to develop bad habits quickly unless professional feedback is available. I suspect this is true in many other subjects, too. The goal is always to optimize learning, and so the decision regarding the use of feedback before practice must be tailored to each situation.

Step Four: Giving Feedback

Students often complain that feedback on assessment is unhelpful or unclear, and sometimes even demoralizing. Students also sometimes report that they are not given guidance in how to use the feedback to improve subsequent performance. Worse still, students sometimes note that the feedback is provided too late to be of any use at all.

On the other hand, faculty members frequently comment that students are not interested in feedback comments and are only concerned with the grade. They express frustration that students do not incorporate feedback advice into subsequent tasks (Spiller, 2009). To illustrate this dilemma, I want to relate the following conversation. I was having lunch at a conference a few years ago when the person next to me began sharing what he and his colleagues had discovered their composition students were doing with all the feedback they received on their writing assignments. If you are a composition teacher, and/or you've ever graded written assignments, you know the amount of time and effort it takes to read and give feedback to students on their writing. He said that in a study conducted with the students in his department, it was found that 50% of the students did not even read the feedback comments, and the other 50% read them but made no effort to incorporate the suggestions into their next writing assignment. The composition teacher I was speaking with had a valid point. Neil Duncan and his colleagues at the University of Woverhampton in the United Kingdom completed a study in 2007 that proved this very point (Duncan, Prowse, Hughes, & Burke, 2007).

I am sure the man I was speaking with at the conference could read the frustration on my face as I thought of the thousands of hours I had spent giving feedback to my students on their writing skills, only to have them ignore it all. I went on to ask him, "Well, what did the department do about these findings?" He explained that they implemented changes that required the students to write a brief summary of all suggested improvements and teacher comments to be submitted to the teacher, thus ensuring the comments had been read. They also suggested that faculty members require students to demonstrate the suggested improvements in future writings or the writing assignments should not be accepted. This story provides an excellent example of educators not only giving feedback but, more important, expecting that the feedback be used. This is a necessary undertaking in an LCT classroom.

Giving meaningful feedback that promotes improved learning is one of the greatest skills of an effective facilitator of education. It is also a skill area where few faculty members have ever had any training. Figure 4.1 lists good feedback principles, developed by Dorothy Spiller in her work *Assessment: Feedback to Promote Student Learning* (Spiller, 2009).

The research on how best to give feedback to students is helpful in designing our own feedback to students. It suggests the following key points:

FIGURE 4.1
Good Feedback Principles

Promote dialogue and conversation around the goals of the assessment task.

Emphasize the instructional aspects of feedback and not only the correctional dimensions.

Remember to provide feedforward: indicate what students need to think about in order to bring their task performance closer to the goals.

Specify the goals of the assessment task and use feedback to link student performance to the specified assessment goals.

Engage the students in practical exercises and dialogue to help them understand the task criteria.

Involve the students in conversation about the purposes of feedback and feedforward.

Design feedback comments that invite self-evaluation and future self-learning management.

Enlarge the range of participants in the feedback conversation to incorporate self-evaluation and peer feedback.

Source: Adapted from Spiller, 2009.

1. The feedback process is most effective when both students and teachers are actively involved in the process. Students often see feedback as the sole domain of the teacher (Taras, 2003).

2. Assessments should be designed so that students can see the direct benefits of attending to the feedback. For example, divide assignments into stages and provide feedback that is essential to completing the next stage. Or give students a provisional grade with opportunity to visit, discuss their work, and potentially earn a higher grade using the feedback.

3. Give feedback that focuses more on instruction rather than correction (Hattie & Timperley, 2007). The message is how to improve.

4. Link feedback to the specific assessment criteria. A rubric is helpful for this step (Nicol & Draper, 2008).

5. Give feedback as soon as possible once students have made every effort to complete the task on their own (Hattie &Timperley, 2007).

6. Use language that the students can understand and that relates directly to the task and its improvement (Duncan, Prowse, Hughes, & Burke, 2007). For example, saying "Expand your synthesis of the issues most pertinent to the outcome of the study" might make sense

to us, but this comment is likely to confuse students. Just as we want them to consider the reader when they are writing, we must think of the receiver of the feedback when we are delivering it.

7. The feedback needs to be very specific to the task and how the task can be improved. Research shows that this type of feedback can have a significant effect on learning enhancement. However, praise, reward, and punishment have little effect on improving learning (Hattie & Timperley, 2007).

8. Feedback should be related to the learning goals. The feedback should reduce the gap between current levels of understanding and performance, and the ultimate learning goal (Hattie & Timperley, 2007). Hattie and Timperley suggest three questions:
   a. Where am I going? *What is my goal for this work?*
   b. How am I going? *What is my progress?*
   c. Where to next? *How do I improve?*

9. A lot of feedback is not always good (Crisp, 2007). Giving feedback and asking that students incorporate it can be more worthwhile if you ask students to choose one part of their work (rather than the whole work) for receiving feedback. This also is a very learner-centered action because it invites more ownership of the feedback process.

Feedback is the key to improved learning. It is the difference between all of the hard work and planning that went into a great teaching activity paying learning dividends and the teaching activity being just a great show. My students cannot know if their annotations are accurate and designed well enough to help their recall unless I tell them or, in some cases, other students tell them. In my class, at least early on, peer feedback is problematic because almost no one knows how to annotate well. My feedback and their application of it is the key to improving their performance.

How Often Should We Give Feedback?

Recall that, in the definition of LCT, I make a specific reference to the context of your teaching situation. That applies here, too. The greater your ability to give well-designed and helpful feedback, the better, but only to the extent that you have the time to assess performance. I give feedback almost daily because my students are in a constant process of building reading skills that are vital to their college success. I suggest you outline a feedback schedule, recognizing that once a month is inadequate but every day may be unmanageable. Students should not have to operate under the illusion that they are "getting it," only to discover after 4 weeks that they were wrong. Regular feedback and the expectation of its use for improvement promote long-term learning. And while promoting long-term learning may not be an essential skill of a teller, it's a fundamental element of an effective facilitator of learning.

It's Not So Hard

For many years I taught a course to future teachers, and I would tell them on the first day that one of the important details that separate highly effective teachers from not-so-effective teachers can be described in one word: files. I would explain that highly effective teachers have hundreds of well-developed lessons that have been tested and work very well to facilitate students' learning; ineffective teachers have none. As you work toward moving your teaching from telling to facilitating, accept that it will take time to develop the files you will need so that students no longer listen passively to a lecture but rather engage in authentic and meaningful work. It can be an enjoyable and creative journey, but it will take some planning, time, and effort to complete.

5

WHO ARE OUR LEARNERS AND HOW DO WE GET TO KNOW THEM BETTER?

We must understand the needs and the beliefs
of our students as they are, not as we think that
they ought to be.

(Rogers & Renard, 1999)

I taught my first class, sophomore English, at an all-girls academy in 1972. As I recall, I was the only male in the building. When I opened my mouth to introduce myself, my voice cracked from nervousness and all the girls laughed. I was embarrassed, but I survived. I went on to get to know the students, appreciate their talents, and gain their trust, and as a result I helped them learn some English literature.

Relating to the Students We Have

What I learned in 1972 was that teaching is in most ways no different than any other human-to-human interaction. If we take the time to get to know our students, respect and value them, explain why we need them to engage in the learning process, and share with them the benefits of learning the subject matter, while proving to them that we have their best interest at heart, then the learning experience is likely to be a very positive one.

This chapter is about the human-to-human interactions that take place in our classrooms every day and how those interactions determine, to a great extent, whether learning is happening. It may be true that some of us learned in spite of our teachers but that was not how we would have liked to learn. Understanding our students and their agendas, attitudes, mindsets, and goals

63

is necessary if we are to create an engaging and exciting learning environment. We must commit ourselves to unlocking the learning potential of the students who sit in our classes and quit wishing for "better" students.

Chapter 5 has three distinct sections. The first section discusses the work of Carol Dweck. Many in higher education are not familiar with her work on the learning mindsets of students. It is among the most important research ever developed in helping teachers to understand the learning behaviors of their students and how teachers may help students change their learning behaviors, leading to greater academic and life success.

The second section in this chapter offers specific strategies for getting to know our students and for building relationships that create mutual trust, respect, and care. If learning in school meets students' emotional needs, they are more likely to engage in the learning. School becomes a motivating place to be (Rogers, Ludington, & Graham, 1998).

The third section in this chapter looks at the work of Spence Rogers and Lisa Renard who, for 15 years, have been developing a model of relationship-driven teaching. This teaching model is based on research that shows the brain does not naturally separate emotions from cognition, either anatomically or perceptually (Caine & Caine, 1994). The emotional centers of the brain are intricately interwoven with the neocortical areas involved in cognitive learning (Zins, Weissberg, Wang, & Walberg, 2004, p. vii). When we become aware of and tend to the emotional needs of students, we enter the realm of learning as well (Rogers, Ludington, & Graham, 1998).

The Mindsets of Our Students

Since the late 1960s, when she was a graduate student at Yale, Carol Dweck has been exploring the mindsets of how students learn. Recently, she put her findings in her book *Mindset: The New Psychology of Success*, written for a lay audience (Dweck, 2006). Her research findings reveal that the students we meet every day in our classes have deep-seated views about their own intelligence and abilities. These views affect their willingness to engage in learning tasks and how much, if any, effort they are willing to expend to meet a learning challenge. These deep-seated views of intelligence fall into two categories, which Dweck refers to as fixed mindsets and growth mindsets (Dweck, 2006, p. 67). In a fixed mindset, students "believe that intelligence is a fixed trait—that some people have it and others don't—and that their intelligence is reflected in their performance" (Dweck, 2006). Many students who believe their intelligence is fixed also believe they either shouldn't need to work hard to do well or putting in the effort won't make any difference in the outcome. In fact, they see putting in effort as sending a signal that they are not smart. They have come to the conclusion that learning just comes easy to smart kids.

A growth mindset is one in which students value hard work, learning, and challenges while seeing failure as something to learn from. In this view, students are willing to take learning risks and understand that, through practice and effort, their abilities can improve. A growth mindset believes the brain is malleable and intelligence and abilities can be enhanced through hard work and practice. These students believe only time will tell how smart they become.

These views of intelligence begin to surface in junior high school, where more stringent academic work appears in the curriculum. Students who could be successful with little effort in elementary school begin to doubt their abilities when the learning challenges increase. Dweck discovered that these students had abilities that inspired learner self-confidence—but only when the going was easy. When setbacks occurred, everything changed. Dweck, with her colleague Elaine Elliott, discovered that the difference between those students who were not put off by the setbacks and those that were put off lie in their goals. "The mastery-oriented students (those with growth mindsets) are really hell-bent on learning something," and learning goals inspire a different chain of thoughts and behaviors than performance goals (Dweck, 2007). Students for whom performance is paramount want to look smart even if it means not learning a thing in the process or putting others down to make themselves look better. For them, each task is a challenge to their self-image, and each setback becomes a personal threat. So they pursue only those activities at which they're sure to shine—and avoid the sorts of experiences necessary to grow and flourish in any endeavor (Dweck, 2007, p. 58).

Dweck is careful to point out that these mindsets are contextual. The same student who believes he cannot do math because he wasn't born with math abilities and that working harder or getting extra help won't help him learn math will take guitar lessons and practice his guitar three hours a day because he knows only practice will improve his playing abilities. Another surprising finding from Dweck's research is that there is no relationship between students' abilities or intelligence and the development of a growth mindset. The explanation for one bright student developing a fixed mindset while another develops a growth mindset has to do with how each student views ability. In the case of a fixed mindset, through misinformation and a lack of input to the contrary from others (including teachers), the student has accepted a belief system that to him makes sense: "The work is getting harder. I must not be all that smart and if I don't have the ability, then effort won't make any difference."

The significance of this research for all of us in higher education is profound. Each fall, tens of thousands of students enroll in classes that they believe they do not have the ability to pass. They also believe that going to tutoring, seeing us in our offices for extra help, or just working harder will make no difference. They hold this belief because their view of their own intelligence is flawed. One of our jobs is to help them recognize that their current level of performance reflects only their current skills and efforts, not their intelligence or worth. We need to correct their misconceptions and get them to see that all of us have the potential to get smarter every day.

Recognizing Our Students' Mindsets

When I first read Carol Dweck's research findings, my mind turned to how I had been viewing my students for many years. I realized that I always saw a lack of effort as laziness and not going to tutoring or coming to my office for extra help as being irresponsible or immature. I realize now that, for many of my students, these behaviors were a direct reflection of their mindsets. They held a belief that they had never been a good reader and nothing was going to change that now. I also recognized that those students who would work hard to improve probably held a completely different mindset than my students who struggled or did not try. They weren't smarter; they just saw themselves differently.

To help us recognize the characteristics of our students' behaviors and attitudes that are displayed in each mindset, I am turning to the work of Michael Richard, who divided the characteristics into six areas for both the fixed mindset and the growth mindset.

Fixed Mindset

1. **Self-image.** Because students see their intelligence as fixed does not mean they don't continue to seek a positive self-image. This action takes the form of wanting to look smart by taking on only easy tasks, trying to make others look dumb, and/or discounting others' achievements.
2. **Challenges.** Students with a fixed mindset often stick to what they know they can do well. Other challenges are to be avoided because

they present a risk to their self-image should they fail. As an advisor, I heard for years students ask, "Are there some easy classes I could take?" This request is likely the sign of a fixed mindset.

3. **Obstacles.** In the case of obstacles, which are defined as things that are external or beyond one's control and therefore harder to avoid, students often make excuses or avoid them by being absent.

4. **Effort.** Students' view of effort is that it is unpleasant and does not pay off in any positive gains; therefore, it is to be avoided. Their perception of what "great effort" is can fall quite short of what is actually required to succeed academically. This may also contribute to their view of effort as futile.

5. **Criticism.** Any criticism of students' abilities is seen as criticism of them at a personal level. Useful criticism is usually ignored or, even worse, seen as an insult. This personal response to criticism leads to less and less chance of improvement because they are not open to using any of the feedback that could help them improve.

6. **Success of others.** Students with a fixed mindset see others' success as making them look bad. They may try to convince their peers that others' successes were due to luck or some objectionable actions. They may even try to distract from the success of others by bringing up their own unrelated personal successes or previous failures of those persons currently successful.

Growth Mindset

1. **Self-image.** Students' self-image is not tied to their abilities because they see their abilities as something that can be further developed and improved. Their desire to learn is paramount.

2. **Challenges.** Challenge is embraced because students believe they will come out stronger for facing it. They believe they will discover valuable information by engaging in the effort.

3. **Obstacles.** Because their self-image is not tied to their success or how they look to others, students see failure as an opportunity to learn. So, in a sense, they win either way. An obstacle is just one more thing on the road of learning and improving.

4. **Effort.** Students see effort as necessary if growth and eventual mastery is to be gained. It is viewed as a natural part of the learning process.

5. **Criticism.** Although these students are not any more thrilled about hearing negative criticism than anyone else, they know it is not personal and that it is meant to help them grow and improve, which

they believe they can do. They also see the criticism as directed only at their current level of abilities, which they see as changing with time and effort.

6. **Success of others.** The success of others is seen as inspiration and information that they can learn from.

Changing Our Students' Mindsets

> A classroom that teaches students to equate their intelligence and their worth with their performance will, in general, stifle the desire to learn and will make students afraid of challenges. After all, the next challenge may show you up and lead you to be branded as less intelligent or less worthy. (Dweck, 2006)

The question that often arises as a result of reading this research is, "Why don't students or their teachers recognize a fixed mindset and do something about it?" From the students' view, as mentioned earlier, they often have no other counsel that might provide a different view, and protecting their self-image is very important. In addition, students can hide this fixed belief by wrapping it in a sense of entitlement and selective self-validation (Atkins, 2007).

Teachers are often unfamiliar with this research and attribute these behaviors to other causes such as laziness or immaturity, as I had done for years. How do we help our students to change their mindsets? Dweck's research, conducted in 2007 with junior high students, offers some important insights. The study involved teaching an eight-session workshop for 91 students whose math grades were declining in their first year of junior high. Forty-eight of the students received instruction in study skills only, whereas the others attended a combination of study skills sessions and classes in which they learned about the growth mindset and how to apply it to schoolwork. Included in the eight sessions was the reading and discussion of an article entitled, "You Can Grow Your Brain." Students were taught that the brain is like a muscle that gets stronger with use and that learning prompts neurons in the brain to grow new connections. From such instruction, many students began to see themselves as agents of their own brain development. Students who had been disruptive or bored sat still and took note. One boy said, "You mean I don't have to be dumb?" The results of the research showed training students to adopt a growth mindset about intelligence had a catalytic effect on motivation and math grades; students in the control group showed no improvement despite all the other interventions (Dweck, 2007, p. 56).

Dweck's research has found that, with students of all ages, from early grade school through college, the changeable view can be taught. Students can be taught that their intellectual skills can be cultivated through their hard work, reading, education, confronting of challenges, and other activities of growth (Dweck, 2007). Dweck explains that students may know how to study, but they won't want to if they believe their efforts are futile. "If you target that belief, you can see more benefit than you have any reason to hope for" (Dweck, 2007). Researcher Joshua Aronson of New York University demonstrated that college students' grade point averages go up when they are taught that intelligence can be developed (Aronson, 2007).

The following are several specific suggestions that Dweck offers about how we can help our students to change their mindsets:

1. *Praise students' effort and strategies, not their intelligence.* Praising students' intelligence, even after great performance, makes them feel good in the short run, but research shows it had many, many negative effects. In contrast, praising students' effort had many positive effects (Dweck, 2007). The dilemma is this: If the praise makes students believe they did well because of their intelligence, what are they to think when they do poorly?

2. *Tell students they can grow their own brains.* Each of us need to share with our students the neuroscience research findings that clearly show new neuron networks are created and become permanent through effort and practice. These new networks make us smarter. This is vital to shifting students away from a fixed mindset. I have detailed much of this information in chapter 1 and on my website, www.learnercenteredteaching.com.

3. *When students fail, focus feedback on having them increase their effort and use improved strategies.* This is a key ingredient in creating growth mindsets. We need to focus our feedback on how students can improve, which usually involves sharing new or different strategies for them to try and strongly suggesting they put forth more effort. The more specific the suggestions we share, the more likely students will improve. If a student gives me feedback that my tests are too hard, it is difficult for me to know what changes to make because the feedback is just too vague. If I am to write a better test, I need specific details about what to change.

4. *Help students understand that their ability to face a challenge is not about their actual skills or abilities; it's about the mindset they bring to*

a challenge. We need to help our students see that taking learning risks and being open to learning all they can from their experiences are most important. This is a difficult message for many students to hear when we have also equated grades with success.

5. *Reinforce in students that current performance reflects only their current skills and efforts, not their intelligence or worth.* Use examples where improvement comes solely from improved technique. Increase your efforts to demonstrate this point.

6. *Offer evidence that students' fixed beliefs are in error, but also teach them the study skills and learning skills they need to succeed in the course.* Teaching students the learning skills needed to be successful in our content areas is a necessary part of helping them see how new skills can lead to improved performance. We can help them to understand that intelligence isn't the issue; they just need some new skills.

What Can Students Do to Help Themselves?

The answer is a lot of self-talk. Carol Dweck offers the following suggestions:

Step 1. Students need to learn to hear their fixed mindset "voice." Students can learn to listen and recognize when they are engaging in a fixed mindset. Students may say to themselves or hear in their heads things like, "Are you sure you can do it? Maybe you don't have the talent." Or "What if you fail—you'll be a failure."

Step 2. Students need to recognize that they have a choice. How they interpret challenges, setbacks, and criticism is their choice. Students need to know they can choose to ramp up their strategies and effort, stretch themselves, and expand their abilities. It's up to them.

Step 3. Students need to talk back to themselves with a growth mindset voice. The fixed-mindset voice says, "Are you sure you can do it? Maybe you don't have the talent." The growth-mindset voice answers, "I'm not sure I can do it now, but I think I can learn to with time and effort."

The fixed-mindset voice might also say, "What if you fail— you'll be a failure." But the growth-mindset voice can answer, "Most successful people had failures along the way."

Step 4. Students need to take growth-mindset action. The more our students choose the growth-mindset voice, the easier it will become for them to choose it again and again (Dweck, 2009).

Building Relationships That Enhance Learning

Students engage in learning when it is meaningful—but meaningful means when the activity satisfies a deep-rooted human emotional need. (Glasser, 1998)

A question one might ask about relationship-driven teaching is, "Can there be any other kind of teaching?" I suspect some might say, "Sure, if you consider that many teachers have little or no relationship with their students but march forward unconcerned, introducing new information, assigning homework and giving tests." In a learner-centered model of instruction, however, relationships play a major role in optimizing students' learning.

Consider these two common learning situations as examples. First, we introduce a new lesson that is difficult and challenging for students, and we know they will struggle with their initial understanding of the material or new skill. In this learning situation, students need to be able to trust that we have their best interest at heart and that we would never put them in a learning situation that was too difficult for them to succeed. What will sustain our students in this difficult learning situation is a trusting relationship that we have nurtured and built over time through deliberate efforts to engage with them on both personal and professional levels. It is the trust that helps them to persevere.

A second example is giving criticism. Let's say that we have just finished checking a major piece of work and are not thrilled with the level of competence displayed or the effort put forth. We recognize the need to give significant amounts of constructive criticism that address both the substance of the work and the effort, or lack of it. The likelihood of our criticism being accepted and valued by our students is tied directly to the relationship we have with them. If they know we care about them and want only for them to improve and reach their potential, then there is great hope that the feedback will be accepted and used to improve future work.

Given the amount of time and effort we put into our teaching, it seems to be common sense that we would want to do everything we could to have our efforts with our students bear fruit. This means creating a learning environment where students want to be because they know they are valued and respected. I am not suggesting that we must be their friends or buddies. After all, how many 18-year-olds want to hang out with a 59-year-old guy who loves to read? I am simply saying that in any human interaction, and especially in one as important as the education of our students, the degree to which there is trust, respect, and caring often determines how much effort one is willing to put forth. If I have no relationship with you, then you are less inclined to do anything for me beyond common courtesies. For example, I have asked dozens of faculty members during my presentations on learner-centered teaching (LCT) if they would give me $20.00. I tell them I could really use the money. Their response varies from a polite no to "Are you crazy?" What's my problem in getting the $20.00? I have no relationship with these faculty members and I have not given them any good reasons to give me the money. The point I am trying to make is that, if I could establish a relationship with them built on respect and trust, they would be more willing to give me the money. And if we were to build a relationship, I would feel the need to give them good reasons for needing the money. This is how our classrooms work, too. If the positive relationship is not in place, the willingness to try, learn, and succeed won't be either.

Using Common Sense in Building Relationships With Students

I taught my first class in 1972. Since then I have learned a few things I think have real value in building relationships with students. The following are my suggestions.

1. *Treat students like they were your son or daughter.* My wife Julie, who coordinates our Hospitality Management Program here at Ferris State University, has used this as her motto for 25 years. She says that it helps her to have more patience and to work to connect on a more personal level with her students. She tells me all the time, "That could be Brendan or Jessica [our kids] sitting there, so I give my students the same level of interest, care, and respect I would give them." How has this motto worked out for her? Since she took over the leadership role, the program has more than tripled in size. Almost daily, she helps students transferring into the program because their roommate or friend told them about the amazing personal interest that the hospitality faculty members show to their students. It has also allowed Julie to give her students much needed criticism about their professional development without them directing resentment or hostility toward her or the program. The results are better prepared graduates whom companies love to hire, with an impressive 98% job placement rate after graduation.

2. *Give students some choice in the learning process.* This is a topic I cover in detail in chapter 6. The key point is that giving students learning choices sends a message of trust in their decision-making abilities, trust in their ability to take responsibility for their learning, and a willingness to let students use their talents (often in ways not found in most syllabi) to demonstrate what they have learned. The result is often discovering the talents that our students have that don't fit traditional assessment measures.

3. *Talk with students one to one whenever possible.* It might sound a bit strange, but I have met many teachers throughout my career who don't like young people. They don't like talking with them or being with them. I guess someone forgot to tell them who they would be teaching when they were hired! One of the easiest ways to build positive relationships with students is just to talk with them. Talk with them before and after class, but also during class. A few minutes of instruction time spent building relationships can go a long way toward improving engagement in the learning process. Students want us to talk with them. They don't always show it, but research says that it's true and that is has academic benefits. In the book *Building Academic Success on Social and Emotional Learning: What Does the Research Say?* by Zins, Weissberg, Wang, and Walberg (2004), the authors show that when we engage with students in building personal and professional relationships in which students can be partners, they not only feel better about the learning process, but they also learn social and emotional skills that aid them in their professional development and increase their academic performance. In addition, it's just plain fun.

   I have always really enjoyed first-year students. I'm not saying that they can't be frustrating, but they are going through so much change that I find a great sense of purpose in helping them make these changes. What do I get for my effort? I get more relaxed learners who enjoy my class and learn that they can become better readers. I know that in the beginning of the semester, my students are not happy to be taking what in their minds is a grade-school–level class in reading. I can either choose to address this attitude and work to connect with them by using humor, stories, personal anecdotes, and assurance that the skills they are being asked to improve are vital to their college success, or I can face a group of grumpy young people three times a week. I vote for the former. Plus, they tell me the most amazing stuff about their lives, and these confidences enhance my joy in teaching. They also write some entertaining things in their papers, like the student who wrote, "Jesus went out from Galilee to teach the genitals." Either he meant "the gentiles," or we were reading different stories!

4. *Care about them personally and educationally.* I do not doubt for a minute that 99% of teachers care about their students and want them to succeed. However, holding that belief inside is different than expressing it openly and often to our students and demonstrating it by our actions. I know my children know I love them, but I also know they need to hear me say it and show it. We need to use this same thought process in our courses. Tell students you value them and demonstrate it by giving them input, choices, and some control over their learning. Listen to their issues and complaints, and appreciate where they are coming from. This doesn't mean you need to give in or lower standards; it just means caring about your students both personally and educationally.

5. *"Never attribute to malice what you can attribute to ignorance"* (Ruggerio, 1995). I was introduced to this concept by Vincent Ruggerio (who has written widely on critical thinking) when he spoke on our campus several years ago. The idea that our students are often unaware that their actions are annoying or out of step with the expected behaviors of college students in a learning environment was something I had not really considered. I recognized that my students in particular were immature in their academic readiness and that immaturity often caused them to behave in ways that were inappropriate for a college learning environment. However, I had never really considered it might be because they didn't know how to behave or that, due to their lack of metacognition or prior knowledge, they didn't understand the social clues that their behavior was inappropriate. This idea changed the way I looked at their behaviors. I began to see each instance of students' behavior issues, both personal and academic, as opportunities to teach them the proper way to behave rather than as reasons to be angry or annoyed with them. I found that when I used each instant as a teaching moment, I not only had better behavior in the class, I also had better relationships with my students. I'm certain that students sometimes act out of malice, but these actions are few. Much more often, students are unaware that

their actions are bothering someone, or they are ignorant of the protocol of the classroom.

Principles of Relationship-Driven Teaching

Spence Rogers and Lisa Renard, in the September 1999 issue of *Personalize Learning Journal*, outlined two basic principles of relationship-driven teaching:

1. Seek first to understand your students. What do they find motivating? What do they believe in?
2. Manage the learning context, *not* the learners. Establish conditions that are likely to foster intrinsic commitments to quality rather than seeking to control students; students will seek to do what needs to be done.

Standards to Meet

Rogers and Renard also set out the following list of standards all teachers need to work toward:

1. *Establish a safe classroom.*
   - Safe from embarrassment and physical threat. If students see you as removing threats, they will feel safe.
   - Only when students feel safe will they take learning risks.
   - Teachers do not penalize themselves when they try new strategies or ideas. We just reteach and try again until we have met our teaching goal. Students need to have dress rehearsal time, too.
2. *Strive to make the work students do be of value to them.*
   - Ask students to find ways in which the information can be used outside the classroom, in real-world applications.
   - Embed the content in activities that students find interesting, like field trips, hands-on simulations, and role-playing scenarios.
   - Brainstorm with the students for ways that the learning can be more pleasant or unique.
   - Find an audience for the students' efforts. Present their work to other classes, people in industry, or other faculty members.
3. *Provide evidence of students' success.*
   - Have students chart their progress.

- Offer clear, meaningful feedback that requires the students to apply the feedback to improve their learning.
4. *Establish a caring classroom.*
   - Smile!
   - Use inviting language: "I would like us all to . . . ."
   - Build community: "We are all in this together."
5. *Use best practices.*
   - Learn how to be a better teacher.
   - Talk with colleagues, read the literature, and use the teaching strategies that you have had success with.
   - Make learning active, authentic, challenging, and meaningful.

We Are All on the Same Team

Teaching is not an us-versus-them competition. Perhaps some days it feels like that, but that feeling won't help optimize our students' learning. We are all on the same team, and we need to communicate that to our students every day. Our goal is simple. We want them to be academically and personally successful, and our promise is to do whatever we can to help them make that happen. Our students need to know we can't make them succeed: Their success will always be up to them. But at the same time, they need to know that we will never act as a barrier to that success. We communicate this support in the relationships we foster.

6

SHARING CONTROL AND GIVING CHOICES

One important rule for helping students learn is to help the learner feel she is in control.

(Zull, 2002)

The first thing our controlling brain sees in a reward or punishment situation is a loss of control.

(Kohn, 1993)

At the 2007 Australian Society for Computers in Learning in Tertiary Education (ASCILITE) Conference, there was an amazing presentation on an authentic learning simulation developed to enhance the preparation of preservice teachers. The presenters' goal for this simulation "was to design a learning environment that allowed for: multiple means of representation, providing learners various ways of acquiring information and knowledge; multiple means of expression to provide learners alternatives for demonstrating what they know; and multiple means of engagement to tap into learners' interests, challenge them appropriately, and motivate them to learn" (Ferry, Kervin, Carrington, & Prcevich, 2007). Or, simply put, the point of the simulation was to give learners choices in how they engaged with the material and control over how they would demonstrate what they had learned. This is learner-centered teaching (LCT) at its best.

Process of Choice

Our students make choices all the time about their learning. They choose to engage in learning or tune it out. They choose to do the assignment or blow it off. They choose to be respectful or disruptive. This chapter is about sharing power with our students. The sharing happens in two distinct ways: by providing choices in the kinds of policies and procedures that will be used in the course, and by giving students more control over what they learn, how they learn it, and how they demonstrate that they have learned.

When we provide students meaningful choices in what and how they learn and more control over how the learning that takes place, we are optimizing their opportunity to choose to engage, participate, share, and work hard at the learning process. New research confirms that having some authority over how one takes in new information significantly enhances one's ability to remember it (Voss, Gonsalves, Federmeier, Tranel, & Cohen, 2011).

The reasons to embrace this sharing process begin with the fact that it is the students' learning, not ours. Yes, we share a responsibility for the learning, but it is not about us; it is, in fact, all about the students. If we are doing what we want to do in the classroom, what is best for us or easiest for us, then we have lost our way as teachers. The classroom has to be about what is best for the learners, even if it is more time-consuming and demanding for us.

It is human nature to want to be in control (Zull, 2002). Evolution has provided us with survival mechanisms that include the ability to take control of our lives. Our students will take control and make choices about their learning no matter what we do. This chapter provides a wide variety of options for giving students choice and control in the learning process that will lead to improved learning. I recognize that many faculty members are not comfortable sharing control over the learning process with their students. Their training was often to the contrary. We were told to keep a tight grip; be firm at first, then maybe loosen up later in the semester. This advice was generated from a them-versus-us mentality. The classroom is seen as a place of confrontation or a struggle for power. The problem with this model is that there have to be winners and losers in any confrontation or power struggle, and 99.9% of the time, the students lose. In an LCT approach, the goal is shared power and increased choices, thus creating a win-win classroom model.

Sharing Power

Figure 6.1 is a list of 16 activities or decisions that take place each semester in almost every course we teach. Review the list and for each item indicate

FIGURE 6.1
Sharing Power

	Teacher	Students	Together	Not Applicable
1. Course textbook				
2. When course exams will be given				
3. Attendance policy				
4. Late work policy				
5. Tardiness policy				
6. Course learning outcomes				
7. Office hours				
8. Due dates for major papers				
9. Teaching methods and/or approaches				
10. Groups formation				
11. Topics for writing or research projects				
12. Grading scale				
13. Discussion guidelines for groups				
14. Rubrics for self-evaluation and evaluation of peers' work				
15. Whether to allow the rewriting of papers				
16. Whether to allow retesting				

if you make the decision (teacher), the students make the decision (students), you and the students make the decision together (together), or the item is not part of your course (not applicable). Although this list may not include every decision that can be made in a course, it does represent most of the important decisions that affect students' learning. After reviewing the list, count the number of decisions you make by yourself (teacher) as an indicator of how much or how little power you share with your students right now. There is no magic number that says, "I share enough" or "I don't share enough." This exercise is simply an opportunity to rethink our decision-making process and determine if there are areas where more power could be shared with our students.

Sharing Builds Community

When we choose to share power with our students by letting them have input in the decisions that affect their learning, several very positive things happen. First, we move our classrooms from us-versus-them to a community of learners. In this environment, responsibility for what happens in the classroom is shared by all. For example, if the policy for turning in late work is decided by us and our students, then we no longer are the enforcer of rules. We get off the hook, so to speak. If a student turns in late work, the consequences for this action were already decided with his or her input. Students must take responsibility for the consequences because they helped to craft the policy. Shared decision making changes the classroom from "I am in charge" to "we are a community." Second, every action we take sends some message to our students. The message that we are willing to share power says that we trust our students to make intelligent decisions that will further their learning and be fair for all. That is a powerful message.

I realize that many people will be uncomfortable sharing power over some of the items in Figure 6.1. My advice is similar to the advice Maryellen Weimer, author of *Learner Centered Teaching*, gave us all in 2002, which was to "go slowly" (Weimer, 2002). I believe we should go slowly, but not too slowly, because the benefits of creating a community of learners outweigh any risks we take or discomfort we might feel. It is also important to note that in each case where we seek students' input, it does not mean we must use it. We have a responsibility to maintain high standards and if the students' input would jeopardize those standards or inhibit learning, then we have every right to say, "Thank you, but the suggested changes cannot be implemented." Feedback that I have received for over 10 years from faculty members who have shared power with their students has been that the students take it seriously, give reasonable suggestions, and are careful to be fair in their actions.

How to Share Power

I have divided the 16 policies and practices in Figure 6.1 into three categories. Each category contains an outline of how to get input from our students specific to each area. Certainly my suggestions are not the only way to proceed, but they have been used by faculty members on campuses across the country for the past 10 years with success.

Category 1: How to Share Power When Forming Course Policies

- Attendance
- Tardiness
- Late work
- Retesting
- Rewriting of papers

The method of sharing power in developing all of these policies is best done using a small-group discussion process. For the students to provide productive input, however, they need clear rationales for why we want to share power with them.

Rationales

- It is their learning, not ours, so they should have a big say in it.
- Sharing creates ownership for the students in their learning experience.
- Sharing power creates community. It moves the classroom away from the teacher-versus-students model.
- Sharing shifts responsibility to the students, where it belongs. They will be responsible for their own learning the rest of their lives and they need to practice that now.

I suspect you can think of other rationales to share, but these will get us started.

Action Steps

1. Introduce the course policies that students are being asked to help write. Usually three to five separate policies can be discussed at one time. Depending on the number of policies, this entire process usually takes between 15 and 30 minutes.
2. Ask the students to form small groups of four to five members.

3. Ask the groups to discuss each policy and give input as to what they feel is fair to students and promotes the learning process. Have the students record their ideas. Students have plenty of experience with these policies and are more than capable of giving meaningful input.

4. After 5 to 10 minutes, ask each group to share its ideas while you record them on the board, computer screen, or flip chart. It is less work getting to a final policy if you record the groups' ideas and display them for all to see.

5. Deal with one policy at a time. After all ideas have been presented for the first policy, have a discussion in which the entire class has an opportunity to give input and the input is recorded. After a few minutes of discussion, move on to the next policy, following the same procedure. It is very possible that multiple versions of a policy will have been developed, giving students' choices when they vote.

6. At this point, you can do one of two things. You can have the students vote on the policies that have been suggested, if clear policies have been determined. The vote should be via secret ballot. If a vote is taken, a simple majority rules. Or you can take all the policy suggestions home and formulate them into well-written policy statements. Then have the students vote the next day class meets. Both are satisfactory actions to take. I personally prefer the latter. Once the voting is complete, the policies are added to the syllabus and become a formal part of the course.

Category 2: Sharing Power on Organizational Issues

- Paper due dates
- Exam dates
- Grading scale
- Topics for papers and projects
- Group formation
- Office hours

Each issue in this category is best handled individually, as they come up during the course of the semester. Either small- or large-group discussion will work.

Assignment Due Dates and Exam Dates

Experience has taught our students that many teachers pick the same time frames for their tests, projects, and/or papers, resulting in an overwhelming amount of work occurring in a very short time frame, usually around the fourth, eighth, and twelfth weeks of the semester. The result is that many of us do not see our students' best work because we have put them in an overload situation that requires them to make choices between which content to study or which paper to write. As a result, neither the test nor the paper is their best work. I realize it is not easy to find times that spread out the work and tests, but if we seek to optimize our students' learning, then spending time discussing assignment due dates and exam dates is really important. Just 10 minutes of class time spent setting optimal due dates and/or test dates can mean improved learning and improved assessment results.

How Grades Are Determined

The message students have heard loud and clear from teachers since they entered first grade is that grades matter. I would like to report that our education systems are moving away from this position, but that would be a big lie. Students know grades can equal graduate school, a better job, scholarship dollars, and bragging rights. So having a discussion about the best ways for students to earn their grades in our courses seems like an important discussion to have. For example, would students rather have more papers and projects or more tests? Would students prefer a test every 3 weeks or every 5 weeks? Every 3 weeks would make the material more manageable, but it also means more tests. The options offered to students will vary from teacher to teacher. The message we give our students when we offer options is that we really do want our students to excel and we are willing to give them input on the most important (to most of them) item in the syllabus: how they will earn their grades.

Topics for Papers or Projects

Whenever possible, we should be giving students choices in what topic they explore as they learn our course material. The reasons are clear. Choice helps improve interest in the topic. Enhanced interest means enhanced engagement. Enhanced engagement likely means a better outcome. In addition, when students choose the topic, they take responsibility for their decision. They cannot blame the teacher for assigning a boring topic. The freedom to choose sends a message that we trust their judgment and respect their ability to learn on their own. These are two powerful messages aimed at boosting students' self-confidence as learners.

How Groups Will Be Formed

The manner in which groups are formed in a course depends on the nature of the work. Researchers suggest three general types: informal groups, which are temporary and often complete their work in a single class period; formal groups, which are formed to complete a specific task and may work together over several class periods; and study teams, which often last the entire semester and serve a variety of learning needs (Davis, 1993). I explore this topic in more detail in chapter 8, but my message here is simple. When appropriate, allowing students to choose their own groups can send a positive message of trust. It puts the students in a position to, as my wife says quite often, "Choose wisely or suffer the consequences." This is a very authentic learning experience.

Office Hours

I met a professor who shared that he held his office hours 10 minutes at a time. For example, students could see him from 10:50 a.m. until 11:00 a.m., four days a week. I asked if he thought that was the best way to help his students. His reply was, "They never come to my office, so I don't know."

In many ways, setting our office hours at times that are best for our students (rather than for us) is the ultimate display of learner-centered teaching. We all know that some of the best learning happens when our students are working one on one with us. The goal here is to optimize one-on-one learning by polling students about the times that are best for them and setting office hours based on this input. Having said this, I realize that there are never any perfect hours, given the schedules students have. We also have lives beyond our teaching and have important reasons for not setting hours at some specific time. However, making an honest attempt to meet students' needs sends a great message that we are willing to do whatever it takes to help them be successful. After all, how many students do we really think will come to our office from 10:50 a.m. to 11:00 a.m.?

Category 3: Teaching and Content Issues

- Textbooks
- Learning outcomes
- Teaching methods
- Discussion guidelines
- Rubrics

Course Textbooks

A revolution is coming in the design of course textbooks. In terms of its arrival, it is not right around the corner but more like a block away. Currently, companies such as Dynamic Books provide faculty members (perhaps with input from students) complete control over course content. Instructors can add, delete, and rearrange chapters and sections. They can upload new material such as links, video, audio, and text files. Dynamic Books provides the ability to change any part of the text. Inkling, a tech start-up founded by former Apple employee Matt MacInnis, is developing interactive text to be used on the iPad. These texts will allow students not only to read about a concept but to connect to a video or website that explains and enhances the understanding of the concept. Course Smart, the e-textbook provider, has come up with an iPad application that allows students to carry all of their textbooks on the iPad; they will be carrying just the tablet to class instead of lugging around an entire backpack filled with heavy paper books.

With all of these new textbook possibilities, it is necessary to involve students in the decision-making process about course textbooks. Given the cost and the dynamic changes that are coming soon in text design, gathering students' input is simply the right thing to do. I know you may be saying to yourself, I can't wait until the course starts to order a textbook. That may be true today, but it is likely to be different in the very near future when books can be downloaded instantly to iPads, smart phones, or other devices, once input from students has been received. For now, we can ask our current students which book(s) they think their peers, who will be taking the course next semester, would find most user-friendly.

Course Learning Outcomes

It may surprise some faculty members that this issue is even on the list, given that learning outcomes have always been the sole domain of curriculum committees and the faculty member teaching the course. I include it because the volume of information available grows at a pace never conceived of even 25 years ago, and we have packed our courses so full that we cannot give equal time to each learning outcome. It is reasonable to present the outcomes to students and ask them which outcomes they feel they will most need our help in reaching and which they can handle with only limited teacher input. Recall that one of the important questions I asked in chapter 3 is, What is the best use of our time? Engaging in a discussion to determine the best use of our time is a good use of our time!

Teaching Methods

Many teachers pick instructional approaches based on how those approaches will help students meet specific learning outcomes. This is what I often do. For example, I may use small groups to facilitate students' learning of course material, but I also use them to help students reach a course learning outcome that deals with organizational skill development. Because of this approach, I do not ask students for their input on what teaching methods they might prefer. However, if the method you use is not linked to a learning outcome, then talking with students about the methods or approaches that help them to learn in the easiest way possible makes good sense. We all know that some students hate group work and others love it. Giving students a choice to work alone or with others is an easy way to share power and optimize their learning. This is also true about giving choices in how learning will be demonstrated. Allowing students to pick the way in which they show what they have learned usually results in a better product.

Discussion Guidelines for Large- or Small-Group Discussions

This topic is covered in detail in chapter 7. When it comes to sharing power in group operation, it makes good sense to get students' input for two important reasons. First, they have been in groups all their lives. They know what makes some groups work and others fail. They have important information to share. Second, if students design the operation of the groups, then they are responsible for getting the groups to work, which is one goal of LCT.

Rubrics for Self-Evaluation or for Evaluation of Peers' Work

When I first began teaching, I asked students questions that I thought would provoke discussion and self-reflection. Here are some of my questions: What do you think about that? How do you see that character evolving? How do you feel about a certain character? Unfortunately, I would hear answers like the following: "It's good." "I like it." "I hate him." "I don't know what *evolving* means."

What I didn't know at the time but learned very quickly was that my students thought that their answers were not only correct but complete. I bring up this personal lesson because we reap two benefits from engaging students in a discussion about what criteria should be used to help them evaluate their own work or that of their peers. The first is that we discover, as I did, what our students know or don't know about what good work is or, in my example, what exactly makes a good answer. Second, we give our students an opportunity to voice what they feel or think quality work entails and how it should be judged. When our students know when their suggestions are good ones, the input will become an element of the rubrics, and there is real incentive for them to take the process seriously. Another advantage of this process is that rubrics designed with students' input at the beginning of the semester add clarity to the expectations we have for our students' work. Students often find this clarity very reassuring and helpful as they work to meet the challenges of the course. This is again a win-win situation.

Students May Resist

Don't be surprised if some students do not want to share power. It's not that they want all the power, but the opposite. They are so conditioned by 12 or more years of teacher-centered education that either they don't feel it is their place to give input, or they just prefer to be told what to do. As we know, the problem with telling students what to do is that it is out of line with the real world of work. Students will be expected to give input; in fact, their input will often aid their advancement. Sharing power is a crucial part of any learner-centered teaching practice. We need to help our students begin the process of taking control of their own learning, even if they don't want to. It will not be the first time we have asked them to do something they didn't want to do and it probably won't be the last. It is very important to their development as lifelong learners, however, that they get started.

7

HOW TEACHERS CAN
FACILITATE STUDENT
DISCUSSIONS BY
NOT TALKING

We can think because we can talk, and we think
in ways we have learned to talk.

(Bruffee, 1984)

Classroom discussion functions best when students are talking to students. Indeed, our goal
is to get as many students involved in talking to
one another as possible and for the teacher to
fade into the background.

(Barton, Heilker, & Rutkowski, 2008)

In chapter 10 of Brookfield and Preskill's book, *Discussion as a Way of
Teaching* (2005), they cite McKeachie (1978) and Bruffee's (1993) findings that so beautifully explain why discussion needs to be a vital part
of a learner-centered teaching (LCT) approach: "Pedagogies that take the
social nature of learning seriously tend to be more successful. Students give
witness that when they have opportunities to discuss, critique, and relate the
material to their own lives, it becomes more meaningful and memorable,
more connected to their understanding of the world." They also report that
when learning is social, and discussion widely used, their educational experiences tend to be more satisfying and more likely to be something they would
choose to reexperience in the future (Brookfield & Preskill, 2005; Mc-
Keachie, 1978; Bruffee, 1993). I read this passage to a colleague of mine and

then asked him why he thought we still have so many teachers who still rely on lecture and use discussion as an afterthought in their teaching approach. His response was, "I have never met a teacher that didn't like to hear himself talk."

Does our desire to hear ourselves and to have others hear us cause us to push aside solid research findings? Brown and Atkins (1988) reported a series of studies by various researchers that found that even with faculty members who try to use discussion, during most of the discussion, the instructor was doing the talking (Brown & Atkins, 1988). In one study, faculty members talked 86% of the time (Brown & Atkins, 1988, p. 53). Is this still true today? I can find no evidence that anything has changed.

Effective Discussions and Learning

This chapter is not about why faculty members should move from lecture to discussion as a teaching approach. Hundreds of studies and books make the case for the learning benefits of discussion (Grasha, 1996; Lowman, 1995; McKeachie, 1994; Nilson, 1996). Compared with the traditional lecture method, discussions elicit higher levels of reflective thinking and creative problem solving, including synthesis, application, and evaluation. There is also evidence that information learned through active discussion is generally retained better than material learned through lecture. Students often prefer to participate in discussions rather than be passive learners in a lecture (McKeachie, 1978). This chapter is about helping students understand that discussion is more than an activity that teachers use on days when they don't have a lecture ready. It is also about how to facilitate effective discussions that enhance students' learning.

Why Students Need Convincing That Discussion Enhances Learning

Most of our students have spent 12 or more years in teacher-centered, traditional classrooms. Although, there are certainly high schools that use a great deal of active learning practices that include well-designed discussion activities, and thousands of individual students who have been involved in discussions that were highly beneficial to their learning, these are unfortunately exceptions to the norm (U.S. Department of Education, 2001). As a result, most of our students have not experienced discussion as a positive learning force in their lives. Many have had experiences where the discussions were nothing more than the teacher talking with two or three students (Karp & Yoels, 1976), or where students just exchanged opinions, often uninformed opinions, and they could not see how the discussion led to any learning. Many of our students see discussion as less than productive. The following are some of the most common reasons:

- Team members see a chance to avoid contributing. They feel they can hide in the crowd and avoid the consequences of not contributing (Latane & Harkins, 1998).
- In large-group discussions, a group member may feel lost in the crowd and unable to gain recognition for his or her contributions (Latane, Williams, & Harkins, 1979).
- In a group discussion, students lose this individuality and the recognition that comes with their contributions. Therefore, these group members lose motivation to offer their full ability because it will not be acknowledged (Charbonnier et al., 1998).
- With so many individuals contributing, some may feel that their efforts are not needed or will not be recognized (Kerr, 1989).
- Students become so-called social loafers. The term *social loafer* describes the phenomenon that occurs when individuals exert less effort when working as a group than when working independently. It begins or is strengthened in the absence of an individual evaluation structure imposed by the environment (Price & Harrison, 2006). This occurs because working in the group environment results in less self-awareness (Mullen, 1983). For example, a member of a sales team will loaf when sales of the group are measured rather than individual sales efforts.
- Concern about evaluation processes also contributes to students' reluctance. If an individual believes compensation has not been allotted equally among group members, he or she will withdraw his or her individual efforts (Piezon & Donaldson, 2005).

For Many Students, Lecture, Not Discussion, Is Equivalent to Teaching

As I visit campuses, I hear two common complaints from faculty members who want to adopt an LCT approach. One is that their department chair has told them they must lecture. "Lecture is how we teach in this department" is the message faculty members receive. The other, more common complaint comes from students who protest to their department chairs that they are not getting their money's worth because "all we do is discuss in our own groups and the teacher never lectures." Both of these complaints have their roots in a teacher-centered approach to instruction. In the case of the department chair who insists on lecture, he or she is out of touch with the research on effective pedagogy and specifically the value of using discussion as an instructional tool. We might want to ask our department chairs to check out Brookfield and Preskill's findings that show discussion helps students become more active, purposeful, and independent learners. Discussion helps participants reach a more critically informed understanding about the topic or topics under consideration, it enhances participants' self-awareness and their capacity for self-critique, it fosters an appreciation among participants for the diversity of opinion that invariably emerges when viewpoints are exchanged openly and honestly, and it acts as a catalyst in helping people take informed action in the world (Brookfield & Preskill, 1999, p. 3).

As for our students, they need a clear set of rationales explaining how discussion will enhance their learning and help them to develop the speaking, listening, and critical thinking skills that are so important to their career success. They will also need to be instructed how to participate actively in a discussion group, which means addressing the concerns I listed a moment ago, especially that of social loafing. Most students have never been instructed how to function in a discussion group unless they have participated in a problem-based learning course or taken a class in small-group dynamics. It is not surprising that our students would find discussion uncomfortable or unproductive if they don't really understand how it works or why they should engage in it.

Rationales for the Use of Discussion

What our students want from us almost daily is to explain *why* we are asking them to read, write, speak, listen, think, and act in the ways we are requesting. They want a reasonable rationale for what they are being asked to do. This should come as no surprise, given that we usually want exactly the same thing from our chairs, deans, or provosts. In the following list, I have included nine rationales for the use of discussion as an effective teaching and learning process. I suspect you can think of others, but these can get you started with your students.

1. Not knowing how to express your ideas in the workplace can be career threatening.
2. Students need to learn that their ideas, suggestions, questions, and concerns will not be heard in the world of work if they wait to be called on. Getting the attention of leadership at any level depends on learning to take the initiative in offering their ideas, suggestions, and concerns.
3. Students need to understand that one of the most important aspects of college learning is hearing the different views of their peers. It is a major way they develop and refine their thinking.
4. Research clearly shows that learning is enhanced by discussion. Students learn more and remember more from their discussion than from lecture (Chickering & Gamson, 1991; Collier, 1980; Cooper & Associates, 1990).
5. The single most important skill students need to be successful in the workplace is the ability to talk and listen to people. In a 1994 survey of more than 11,000 college graduates, the most important life skill (out of 16 choices, including critical thinking) was interpersonal skills (Cooperative Institutional Research Program, 1995). Talking and listening are also the two activities they will do most often during any given workday. Discussion helps build these important skills.
6. Most work in the real world is done in teams and groups. Learning how to get along and collaborate in small and large discussion groups is great practice for this, especially if a student is not naturally outgoing or prefers to work alone.
7. Discussion develops critical thinking skills. It is vital to be able to practice the thinking skills of analysis, synthesis, and evaluation in a safe environment, which a classroom discussion affords. The classroom is where we want our students to make their mistakes, not in the real world. This is a very important rationale, one that needs to be repeated often.
8. Challenging or affirming others is important in effective communication. Discussion is a chance to practice the skills of disagreement, confrontation, and affirmation—are all vital to our students' long-term success.
9. Discussion allows students the opportunity to clarify their thinking and organize their thoughts. James Zull, in his book, *The Art of Changing the Brain*, discusses what he calls the natural learning cycle (Zull, 2002, p. 18) of the brain, which follows quite nicely David

Kolb's experiential learning model (Kolb & Fry, 1975). In both models, the final step in processing information is to test it. To make the information public, in the case of discussion, students must speak the words. Only then can students really know if what they are thinking makes sense because only then can others give them feedback. Our students need to understand that they must discuss their thinking to know if it makes sense, can be improved, or is the best way to solve a problem.

Designing Effective Discussions

Students who can see each other and share the same collaboration space experience far superior communication as they are exposed to gaze, gesture and nonverbal behaviours. (de Byl, 2009)

From almost the first day our students entered school, they learned that the teachers have the answers and the teachers will tell them what to learn and how to learn it. They also learned that the teachers enjoy having the answers and many enjoy sharing the answers with them. We now know that this teacher-centered process actually diminishes learning because it reduces the active role of learners in seeking and finding answers for themselves. This knowledge about teachers—that they have the answers—often serves to impede effective discussion. Our students know that if they remain quiet or act as if they don't understand, most teachers will come charging to their rescue and provide the answers. As a result, students have learned to wait during discussions, knowing that most teachers can't stand silence and will break the silence by providing the answers.

In a learner-centered teaching approach, one of the important changes we have to remember in our interactions with our students during discussions is to *keep our mouths shut* as much as possible. If our students know that we will not rescue them, we can handle the silence, and we expect the discussion to be handled by the students and by them alone, they will take up the task. It may take a while for them to accept that we are not going to give them the answers, but they will get the message.

Getting Students' Input on the Design of the Discussion

One thing our students have learned over their 12 or more years in school is what makes a discussion, whether in a large or small group, work and not work. They have experienced firsthand terribly boring discussions and exciting, learning-filled ones. As we know, one goal of an LCT approach is to share power with our students. The design, including the guidelines, of a discussion is a perfect place to share power. We need to get our students' input on what makes a great discussion and what ruins one, and then use this information to design the discussions and the guidelines for making them work.

Ground Rules for Discussion—Students' Input

I developed this process using advice from Maryellen Weimer's book, *Learner Centered Teaching: Five Key Changes to Practice* (Weimer, 2002). I have used the process many times and have been recommending it to faculty members for over 12 years. The most meaningful things we can do is to explain to students that their input will be used to design the discussions for the course.

Step 1. Have students meet in groups of three and discuss:

1. What are the characteristics, behaviors, environments, guidelines, topics, and questions that made for some of the best discussions you have been a part of in your past learning?
2. What are the characteristics, behaviors, environments, guidelines, topics, and questions that made for the worst discussions?

Step 2. Ask the oldest student to be the recorder for the group. Have all responses recorded. Ask the youngest student to be the spokesperson for the group.

Step 3. Have each group share its answers with the class. An effective way to do this is to ask each group to share just one answer each time that group is called on, until all answers have been shared by all groups. This allows everyone to have an equal opportunity to share meaningful ideas. This promotes a sense of community.

Step 4. Record all answers in a Word document if possible (or on the board), separating the responses on what makes discussions work from what causes discussions to fail. Be certain that everyone can see all the responses.

Step 5. Have the students remain in their groups but divide the class in half. Have one half use the list of ideas on what makes discussions work and the set of questions found in Figure 7.1 to guide their

FIGURE 7.1
Questions for Student Discussion of Guidelines

- Who gets to participate in the discussion? Must students have read the assignment or completed the homework? If so, how will this be verified?
- How do students participate in the discussion? Do they raise their hands and then are acknowledged by the professor? Do they just speak out when they have something to ask or add? Does everyone need to take part in the discussion? Can students speak as many times as they want?
- Because challenge and disagreement are healthy parts of a discussion, what behaviors are acceptable when students challenge or disagree with one another so that the discussion remains civil and productive?
- What language will be deemed inappropriate for classroom use based on current cultural norms?
- How should students be graded? Should they be graded on their participation in the discussion? If they are graded, do all responses (e.g., asking a question, giving a view, challenging an answer, expanding on an answer, etc.) count the same?
- What are the consequences for those who do not participate?
- Should there be a privacy rule that anything discussed in the classroom stays in the classroom?
- Who should be responsible for recording responses?

thinking. These students develop what they believe would be an effective set of guidelines for conducting class discussions. Ask them to write with clarity what each guideline would be. Have the other half of the class use the ideas on what makes groups fail and the set of questions in Figure 7.1 to develop guidelines that would prevent effective class discussions from happening. For example, if a problem with discussion is one person dominating the discussion, the guideline might be that no one can talk more than three times until everyone who wants to speak has had their say.

Step 6. Repeat Step 3, combining and refining suggestions, with the goal of reaching a master list of guidelines.

Step 7. Inform the students that you will take all of their suggestions, incorporate them into a master list for the class, and bring the master list to the next class for a vote. Also inform them that you may add ideas if you think they are necessary to the development of an effective set of guidelines and that you may also choose to veto a student suggestion if you view it as detrimental to an effective discussion.

Step 8. Let the students review the guidelines and then conduct a secret-ballot vote to determine their acceptance. I have never had a vote of *no* on the guidelines, but if this were to occur, you could ask the students to discuss again which pieces may need revising. In Appendix A, you will find several sample sets of guidelines that you may find helpful in establishing guidelines for your own class. Examples of both large- and small-group guidelines are included.

Facilitating an Effective Group Discussion

Teachers have multiple conceptions of classroom discussion, but these conceptions often intersect with two purposes for using classroom discussion: (1) Discussion is seen as a method of instruction, where the purpose is to help engage students in a lesson and to help them learn academic content by encouraging verbal interactions; and (2) discussion competence is the subject matter, where the desired outcome is for students to learn to discuss more effectively (Larson, 2000). The key to effective facilitation is in the planning, whether one or both of these outcomes are the desired goals for discussion.

With an effective set of guidelines in place (thanks to the help of our students), the success of the discussion turns to three important design factors. First, what kind of discussion do we want to have? The choices are small groups of two, three, four, or more students, or a large group where all or most of the students take part. The decision depends on our learning outcome and on how well we have prepared our students to be active participants in a discussion. My only caution about using small groups—and it only concerns working with first-year students and comes solely from my own experience—is that you may want the keep the groups smaller rather than larger. I use only groups of two because it is very difficult to get lost in a group of two and everyone usually gets to contribute. My reasoning is that, because my students are coming from a very teacher-centered high school experience where group work may not have been a positive part of their learning experience, I need to stack the odds in favor of success by putting them in a social and academic situation that is easier to handle. I also do this so students might make a friend or at least a connection with someone else in the class, which is helpful in building community in the classroom.

The second design factor is deciding what will be discussed. What is the topic, question, problem, case, idea, reading, film, and so on that students will be talking about? What is the learning outcome(s) we want to have from this discussion? In other words, what do we anticipate our students learning from the discussion? In planning this part of the design, it is crucial to prepare well-conceived questions that reflect the learning outcomes and are within the ability levels of our students' thinking processes. As a faculty developer for 12 years, I worked with many faculty members who overshot the thinking abilities of their students or failed to see the limits of their students' background knowledge and ended up with useless discussions. We cannot ask our students, for example, to evaluate findings or outcomes from research unless they have the expertise to do so and unless we have taught them how to perform evaluations. Failure to know the ability levels and prior knowledge of our students has doomed many a discussion.

Well-Conceived Questions

Questions calling for factual recall are the type of questions that are least likely to promote student involvement. In contrast, studies show that open-ended questions calling for divergent thinking (i.e., questions that allow for a variety of possible answers and encourage students to think at a deeper level than rote memory) are more effective in promoting discussion than closed questions calling for convergent thinking (one correct answer) (Andrews, 1980; Bligh, 2000). Ironically, and fortuitously, these results indicate that students are more likely to respond to questions that require deeper-level thought (critical thinking) than rote memory (Gardiner, 1994). Brookfield and Preskill (2005) propose several types of questions that promote effective discussion, including questions that ask for more evidence, questions that ask for clarification, open-ended questions, linking or extension questions, hypothetical questions, cause-and-effect questions, and summary and synthesis questions.

Metacognitive questions, which are designed to help students construct their own meaning through self-questioning, are also effective. Four types of inquiry can be posed: (1) What is your comprehension of the problem? (2) Are there connections between former and current problems? (3) What strategies did or would you use to solve the current problem? and (4) Reflect on the process used and the results of using that process (Mevarech & Kramarski, 2003). The possibilities are endless. However, the key is that the questions directly reflect the learning outcomes, are able to be answered in the time frame given, and are at appropriate thinking levels. Consulting Bloom's taxonomy (Bloom & Krathwohl, 1956) or Bloom's revised taxonomy (Anderson & Krathwohl, 2001) is an excellent way to ensure that our questions match the thinking levels where we want our students to be working. Bloom's revised taxonomy, along with suggested verbs to help in writing questions, appears in Figure 7.2. Figure 7.3 provides examples of questions and tasks that might help discussions to be highly productive in the sciences and other research areas. Internet searches will lead to many other well-written discussion questions in a variety of content areas.

Discussion Methods

The third design factor is the discussion method(s) to be used. Methods can vary greatly and depend again on the learning outcomes and the level of readiness students have for participating in a discussion. Listed here are a few examples. Many more can be found by searching "discussion strategies" or "discussion methods" on the Internet.

1. **Guided discussions.** In this discussion, the teacher poses questions designed to lead the students toward a particular outcome. This

FIGURE 7.2
Bloom's Revised Taxonomy

Remembering: Can the student recall or remember the information?
(Verbs: define, duplicate, list, memorize, recall, repeat, reproduce, state)

Understanding: Can the student explain ideas or concepts?
(Verbs: classify, describe, discuss, explain, identify, locate, paraphrase, recognize, report, select, translate)

Applying: Can the student use the information in a new way?
(Verbs: choose, demonstrate, dramatize, employ, illustrate, interpret, operate, schedule, sketch, solve, use, write)

Analyzing: Can the student distinguish between or among the different parts?
(Verbs: appraise, compare, contrast, criticize, differentiate, discriminate, distinguish, examine, experiment, question, test)

Evaluating: Can the student justify a stand or decision?
(Verbs: appraise, argue, defend, evaluate, judge, select, support, value)

Creating: Can the student create a new product or point of view?
(Verbs: assemble, construct, create, design, develop, formulate, write)

Source: Overbaugh & Schultz, 2008.

FIGURE 7.3
Research-Related Questions and Tasks

1. State the study's major findings.
2. Explain the meaning and importance of the findings.
3. Relate the findings to those of similar studies.
4. Consider alternative explanations of the findings.
5. State the clinical relevance of the findings.
6. Acknowledge the study's limitations.
7. Make suggestions for further research (Hess, 2004).
8. Defend your answers, if necessary, by explaining both why your answer is satisfactory and why others are not.
9. Discuss and evaluate conflicting explanations of the results.
10. Discuss any unexpected findings.
11. Identify potential limitations and weaknesses, and comment on the relative importance of these to your interpretation of the results and how they may affect the validity of the findings.
12. Summarize concisely the principal implications of the findings, regardless of statistical significance.
13. Explain how the results and conclusions of this study are important and how they influence our knowledge or understanding of the problem being examined.

Source: Hess, 2004.

method has a lot of structure and takes thoughtful planning to execute well.

2. **Debate.** Students will need some instruction on how the debate format will be used in class. A wonderful resource for this can be found at http://www.rci.rutgers.edu/~jhudson/takingsides.html, where Dr. Judith Hudson has detailed the debate process for students. The topic for the debate can be assigned or chosen by the students. Students research and/or read about the different positions surrounding the topic, either on their own or using assigned materials. Following the format for the debate, students engage in meaningful exchanges leading to new insights (one hopes) about the topic.

3. **Role play.** Role play can take many forms, but the key ingredient is that it allows students to move outside themselves, shedding some of their own insecurities. It also helps them to understand more deeply how others think by assuming a new identity, even if it is just for a little while. Students can choose their own roles or they can be assigned. Students then research the roles so they may be prepared

to express the views of their assumed identity. Variations on this method include assigning roles to students as they walk into class (handing each student a card with a role on it as they enter the classroom or sending them their role online) and having them respond to discussion questions through the eyes of the assigned role.

What to Do After the Discussion Ends

The research on memory formation clearly shows that it takes both repetition and elaboration over time to form long-term memories (Schacter, 2001). Chapter 10 discusses this topic further. The learning that results from a discussion depends to a great extent on what we ask our students to do with the new insights, understanding, facts, and concepts after the discussion ends. One of the great failures of the discussion method is the lack of follow-up activities that ask students to practice or apply their new knowledge. The students walk away enthusiastic about the discussion if it went well, but that is often the end of it. If we are to optimize our students' learning from discussion, we must give them additional work to help the learning become more long-lasting. The following are some suggestions:

1. Have students write reflection papers. Reflection is the lost art of academia. We are in such a hurry to get all the content covered that we rarely make time for one of the most important ways in which humans learn. Since Dewey first wrote about reflection in *How We Think: A Restatement of the Relation of Reflective Thinking to the Educative Process* (Dewey, 1933), teachers have known that reflection leads to new connections with prior knowledge and creates improved understanding with better recall of the information. A reflection paper can have many uses because it allows students to focus on how they can apply what they have learned in the discussion to other parts of the course or areas of their learning at the university, or how the new learning affected their lives on a personal level. The key is to have it reflect the learning outcome for the discussion.

2. Have students write a summary of what they learned from the discussion. This assignment has multiple benefits. First, it demonstrates what the students thought was important from the discussion, which can then be compared to what the teacher thought was important and thus reveal possible gaps in the students' learning. Second, if students know they will be asked to summarize, they'll know that they will need to take notes and listen carefully to the discussion,

both effective for learning. Third, summaries are written in the students' own words and therefore reveal how well they understood all that was discussed. If students can't translate new knowledge into their own words, it is a sign that they had difficulty with their comprehension. This is important for teachers to know.

3. Request that students make a fact or idea sheet listing all of the new information they gained from the discussion. In this activity, students simply list new ideas, facts, and concepts or fresh ways of looking at an idea that they learned during the discussion.

4. Make a mind map of the discussion. Mapping is a great learning tool because it requires students to identify the major ideas and important details about those ideas in a visual format. This causes them to make judgments about what was important and what details supported those ideas, again important for teachers to know. An additional plus to this type of assignment is that visual images are among the easiest for the human brain to learn (Zull, 2002, p. 137). Having students make visual displays is all the better for their learning.

Assessing Discussions: Both Skill Development and Content Knowledge

Treat Discussion Knowledge Just Like Lecture Knowledge

Another area of failure in discussion planning is the lack of meaningful assessment of what was learned from the discussion. If we are using discussion as a tool for learning, we must assess what our students have learned in formal ways. The kind of assessment I am talking about is not the grading of an individual discussion activity or the giving of participation points that are factored into the final grade. I discuss these later in the chapter. Both are certainly forms of assessment, but they don't usually reflect whether the learning outcomes for the discussions were met. What I am strongly suggesting is that we must design formal ways to determine what was learned from the discussion. The following are some suggestions:

1. Test students on discussion material just like you test them on lecture material. Helping students to know what to study can be accomplished in two ways. One is to have the students develop a wiki site for the class discussions. At this site, students can post what they think was important to know from the discussions. A wiki allows for

easy editing, so incorrect information can be changed easily. You will have access to this site, too, so you may check that the students have identified all the material they will need for the test. The use of a wiki site is a learner-centered activity that reduces the use of class time for reviews. A second solution is to provide students review sheets that identify what students will need to know for the test. Review sheets are more teacher-centered tools than is a wiki, but they are still effective.

2. Assign papers designed to show what students have learned from a set of class discussions.

3. Ask students to make presentations using material learned from discussion. In their presentations, they solve a problem, demonstrate their understanding of a concept, or apply new knowledge to the course outcomes.

Unless we assess what our students have learned from discussion in formal ways, we send a message that discussion is less valuable than other learning in the course. This kind of message only reinforces what many students already believe about discussion: that it is not that important.

Should We Grade the Improvement of Discussion Skills?

If we are trying to measure whether students have improved their abilities to participate in active and effective ways in large-group classroom discussions, and if improving these behaviors is a learning outcome for the course, then the answer to the question posed in the heading is yes. Devising an effective grading system is another story. Here are a couple of suggestions:

1. Write each student a note at midterm and at the end of the semester apprising her or him of her or his grade. Give clear feedback on the progress each student made in improving her or his discussion skills. This would likely require a rubric (see the example in Figure 7.4).

2. Record each time a student contributes. Use a simple code, for example, M for meaningful contribution, S for satisfactory contribution, and T for talked but contributed little to the discussion. Use the record to track improvement and decide what grade each student receives.

Grading Small-Group Discussion Skills

If we are seeking to grade small-group discussion in terms of improved discussion skills, the task is even harder. The model used most often combines

FIGURE 7.4
Collaborative Work Skills: Group Discussion

Category	4	3	2	1
Focus on the task	Consistently stays focused on the task. Very self-directed.	Focuses on the task most of the time. Group members can count on this person.	Focuses on the task some of the time. Other group members must sometimes remind the student to keep on-task.	Rarely focuses on the task. Lets others do the work.
Contributions	Routinely provides useful ideas. Contributions are clear and well organized.	Usually provides useful ideas. Contributions are mostly clear and well organized.	Sometimes provides useful ideas. Contributions are not always clear or well organized.	Rarely provides useful ideas. Contributions are rarely clear or well organized.
Working with others	Almost always listens to, shares with, and supports the efforts of others.	Usually listens to, shares with, and supports the efforts of others.	Often listens to, shares with, and supports the efforts of others.	Rarely listens to, shares with, and supports the efforts of others.
Attitude	Never is publicly critical of the project or the work of others.	Rarely is publicly critical of the project or the work of others.	Occasionally is publicly critical of the project or the work of other members.	Often is publicly critical of the project or the work of other members.
Ground rules	Abides by all of the ground rules established by the class.	Abides by most of the ground rules established by the class.	Abides by a few of the ground rules established by the class.	Does not abide by the ground rules established by the class.

the use of rubric-guided peer review and self-review along with a grade on the group's work. This model leaves something to be desired because the grade on the work is not a direct reflection of the individual's discussion skills. Another alternative, which is labor-intensive, is to observe the groups in action and meet with each individual member, or all members together, two or three times over the semester to discuss their progress in improving their discussion skills. Sharing constructive feedback with students on what improvements you expect to see in their discussion skills and grading their existing performance (refer again to Figure 7.4) sends a clear message that you want them to work on improving their skills. In the end, the reality of our individual teaching assignments will dictate what assessment process is most appropriate.

Points for Participation

I estimate that I have sat in at least 200 conference breakout sessions over 34 years and at least a third of them dealt in some way with how to conduct effective discussions. In these sessions, the conversation always gets around to grading students' participation. The suggestions about how to do this vary greatly, and I often find them unsatisfying because they either require a lot of record keeping or a lot of subjective judgment about the quality of a contribution a given student might make. How to reward participation, if indeed it should be rewarded, is a topic we should let students consider when they develop the guidelines for the discussions at the beginning of the semester. Note that participation points send the message that students are being rewarded for doing what they should be doing anyway as an active learner in our courses. Participation points also reward some students who have better speaking skills, are more outgoing, or like to hear themselves talk, sometimes at the expense of students who may be shy or are more reflective and thoughtful about what they say and therefore speak less often. My point is that assigning points based on participation is a difficult process to get right.

Facilitating Takes Practice

In researching this chapter, I found entire books written on the topic of effective facilitation. It is clearly not an easy role to take on and takes some practice to do effectively. The one theme that ran through all of the books and articles on this topic was that effective facilitators let the students do as much of the work—talking, struggling, wrestling, and collaborating—as possible. Roger Schwarz's *The Skilled Facilitator* (2002) offered the following suggestions:

1. Recognize that each action sends a message, so planning is vital to success.
2. Have a clear mission or learning outcome.
3. Understand the group culture.
4. Make certain the tasks are appropriate to the ability level of the learners.
5. Define the roles of the members or learners.
6. Allow sufficient time to complete the task. (Schwarz, 2002, p. 19)

If we follow this advice and accept that there will be some bumps in the road, we should do just fine.

8

TEACHING TO
ALL THE SENSES

Our senses work together so it is important to
stimulate them! Your head crackles with the perceptions of the whole world, sight, sound, taste,
smell, touch, energetic as a frat party.

(Medina, 2008)

As I wrote earlier, I like to teach first-year students. I realize that not
everyone in higher education would agree, but I find first-year students interesting, open, and looking for a connection to the university that I can provide. I feel like I'm needed. I suspect because of this, I get
assigned to teach a course (Directed Studies Seminar 100) that I fondly call,
"I should have studied harder 100." This is a class for students who are on
academic probation and in need of help in a multitude of areas, including
study habits, time management, sleep and nutrition, and attitude correction.

The Learning Experience

One of the lessons I teach in this course deals with why the human brain
needs proper nutrition, exercise, oxygen, sleep, and hydration to function at
its best. As part of this lesson, I demonstrate how much sugar there is in a
20-ounce bottle of Coca-Cola (15 teaspoons) and how much fat there is in a
Burger King Whopper hamburger (40 grams) as a way to suggest to students
that they might want to make better choices in feeding their brains. Because
I believe their nutrition may have played a role in their being on probation
(poor attention and focus, low energy, getting ill more often), I want to
make certain my students remember my message about sugar and fat, so I
use a very multisensory approach to teach them. I bring to class a sugar bowl

To view chapter-related videos please go to tinyurl.com/learnercenteredvideo.

filled with sugar, a few silver teaspoons, Crisco shortening, and two clear 8-ounce glasses. I begin filling a glass with sugar, one teaspoon at a time, asking the students to tell me to stop when they think I have put the same amount of sugar in 20 ounces of Coca-Cola into the glass. Without fail, they stop me several times before I get to 15 teaspoons. I hold up the glass so my students can see how much sugar they take in when they drink 20 ounces of Coca-Cola: The 8-ounce glass is nearly one-third full. I don't stop with just this visual display. I then pass the glass around the room and ask each student to take a close look at the amount of sugar and to feel its weight. When the glass is returned to me, I take a teaspoon, fill it with sugar, stick it in my mouth, and swallow it. The students actually cringe at seeing this. I then take another spoon and ask for volunteers to eat a spoonful. I rarely get any. I point out that I ate only one spoonful and everyone was cringing, yet we will drink 15 teaspoons of sugar while having lunch with little thought or concern. If this were not enough, I then take out a can of Crisco shortening and begin filling the other 8oz glass with 40 grams of shortening, the amount of fat in a single Whopper hamburger. I again ask them to tell me when they think I have 40 grams (40 grams = 0.0883002 pounds). After arriving at the 40 grams, I repeat the same process of passing the glass around the class. When it is returned, I take out another spoon, fill it with the shortening and begin to put it on my mouth. Absolute horror appears on many of my students' faces until I stop right before the spoon enters my mouth. They get the message loud and clear.

This use of a multisensory teaching process, combined with the emotional arousal it causes, has resulted in almost every student listing this lesson as one of the most important and unforgettable in the course on the end-of-semester evaluation. When I run into my students in future semesters and ask them about their Coca-Cola drinking or Whopper eating, most say, "I rarely do that anymore."

Research on the Power of Multisensory Teaching and Learning

Our results show that multisensory interactions can be exploited to yield more efficient learning of sensory information and suggest that multisensory training programs would be most effective for the acquisition of new skills. (Seitz, Kim, & Shams, 2006)

The eyes, nose, ears, tongue, and skin contain sensory receptors, which are specialized nerve endings that act as sense detectors. Sensory receptors transfer detected stimuli to regions of the brain that allow people to perceive the sensory information. The auditory cortex, visual cortex, and sensory cortex are regions of the brain dedicated to sensory perception (Mackay, 1999). In the scientific community, perception has traditionally been viewed as a modular function, with the different sensory modalities operating largely as separate and independent systems. However, recently accumulating reports of cross-modal interactions in various perceptual tasks and settings suggest that interactions between modalities are the rule rather than the exception in human processing of sensory information. Recent neurophysiological studies of cross-modal interactions provide evidence for these interactions occurring at early stages of perceptual processing in brain areas that have long been viewed as modality-specific (Seitz, Kim, & Shams, 2006). Considering that cross-modal interactions are ubiquitous in human perceptual processing and that they play some role in the development of perceptual processes, it is likely that multisensory interactions may be exploited to render the processing of sensory information more effective in terms of encoding and learning as well (Seitz, Kim, & Shams, 2006). The translation of this important finding is that our senses work together, not in isolation, as was once thought, and when multiple senses are used in instruction, better encoding of information takes place, thus allowing for improved recall of the information. People in multisensory environments always do better than those in unisensory environments. They have more recall with better resolution that lasts longer, evident even 20 years later (Medina, 2008). It is interesting to note that this recent scientific finding, which affirms the value of using a multisensory approach to instruction, confirms what those of us who work with students with learning disabilities, especially in the areas of language development, reading, and math, have been doing for a century. In this case, we guessed right.

This chapter deals with how to use a multisensory approach to enhance the learning of our students. It explores how to help our students to use this technique in their own learning and how we can improve our teaching by integrating these methods into our instructional practices.

Helping Students Become Multisensory Learners

You might think that telling our students about the numerous studies proving that a multisensory approach to learning improves understanding and recall would be enough to get them to stop trying to memorize everything. However, old habits die hard. Our students have been using the same methods to study for years and are not easily convinced they should change.

Chapter 11 of this book discusses research that clearly shows how exercise significantly improves learning. In fact, it may be the most important thing students can do to improve their learning (Ratey, 2008). I have been sharing this information with my students since it came out in 2008, but I have not found them running over to the gym to exercise. Students take a lot of convincing. The following sections discuss research findings that demonstrate the power of a multisensory approach to learning. I am including them as rationales to use with students to get them to abandon their memorize-only methods of study.

Hear and See

The following findings are from a study that compared the recall of information delivered using unisensory methods to the recall of information delivered via multisensory methods. The period between presentation of the material and the testing for recall was 2 weeks. Those who:

- Only read the information were able to recall 10% of it.
- Only heard the information were able to recall 20%.
- Only saw the information were able to recall 30%.
- Both heard and saw the information were able to recall 50%. (Dale, 1969)

See and Touch

In a study done in 2003, learners were compared on their recall of correct answers using the sense of touch alone, sight alone, and touch and sight combined. In these findings, we can once again see the advantage of a multisensory approach.

Sight and touch   85% correct
Touch only   65% correct
Sight only   72% correct (Newell, Bulthoff, & Ernst, 2003)

Several studies have shown that students who took in new information using more than one sensory pathway produced 50% more creative solutions to the problems they had been assigned (Mayer & Anderson, 1992).

Smell

The olfactory area governs the sense of smell. Located in the orbitofrontal cortex, just above the eye socket, the olfactory area is associated with the limbic system, or areas of the brain that govern emotion. For that reason, specific odors can evoke powerful emotional responses (Mendonca, 1997). Because of this finding by Mendonca, I strongly encourage my students to use the sense of smell to help them recall what they have been studying. I usually begin by asking the students what smells they like. I encourage them to find a smell and use it when studying and then bring it to class to help their recall. I do need to warn you that what we think of as a useful smell for learning and what our students think of can be quite different. One of my student's favorite smell was deer urine (we have hundreds of students who are deer hunters at our university), so I strongly suggested he bring a different smell to class.

The part of our brain that handles smell—the piriform cortex—is located directly next to the part responsible for memory and emotion. This has led to our memories becoming intrinsically and strongly linked with odor. Smell can evoke the emotions surrounding an experience, and it can prompt and even re-create those emotions. A growing body of research shows that smell can be used to improve recall because of the link between smell and emotions. Students who learn in a room infused with the scent of rosemary or lavender are able to remember far more information when they encounter that smell again (Microsoft Training, 2010).

The key is that the smell needs to be congruent with the learning task. Foul smells, for example, can evoke many different emotional memories that might interfere with the recall of the information. Students want a smell they like and can positively associate with what they are learning. In a study published in 2010, researchers May O. Lwin, Maureen Morrin, and Aradhna Krishna found that, after a time delay, scent enhances recall of verbal information, and scent-based retrieval cues potentiate the facilitative effect of pictures on recall, too (Lwin, Morrin, & Krishna, 2010). A Harvard University study appearing in the *Journal of Science* in 2007 showed that volunteers who were exposed to bursts of rose scent as they slept after studying were better able to recall the material, even without being exposed to the scent again. The odor intensified the transfer of information to the hippocampus, the part of the brain responsible for forming longer-term memories (Rasch, Buchel, Gais, & Born, 2007).

Pictures and Images: The Power of Seeing

In a 1998 study, students were found to have three times better recall of visual information over oral information, and six times better recall when the information was presented using oral and visual information at the same time (Najjar, 1998). Humans are incredible at remembering pictures. Hear a piece of information, and three days later you'll remember 10% of it. Add a picture and you'll remember 65% (Medina, 2008). If we think about vision from an evolutionary perspective, it makes perfect sense that the human brain would have been well developed to see things in order to survive. Seeing was necessary for finding food, predators, and a mate (Medina, 2008). Images are the easiest thing for the brain to learn (Zull, 2002). We need to help our students to understand this and to develop learning processes where they may regularly translate information into images (e.g., graphs, charts, maps, pictures, drawings) as a way of improving understanding and recall.

Teaching Using a Multisensory Approach

Using a Multimedia Approach

People learn better from words and pictures than from words alone (Mayer, 2009). This summarizes the promise of multimedia learning. However, simply adding words to pictures is not an effective way to achieve multimedia learning. Psychologist Richard Mayer developed a cognitive theory of multimedia learning (Mayer, 2009). He suggests there are three main assumptions when it comes to learning from multimedia:

1. There are two separate channels, auditory and visual, for processing information. This is sometimes referred to as dual-coding theory (Paivio, 1986).
2. Each channel has a finite capacity. This is called the cognitive load theory (Sweller, 1988). It means the channels can be overloaded when learners are bombarded with too much information. A teacher can push students' cognitive load by putting an excessive amount of material on a PowerPoint slide, for example.
3. Learning is an active process of filtering, selecting, organizing, and integrating information based on prior knowledge.

Humans can process only a limited amount of information in a channel at a time, and they make sense of incoming information by actively creating mental representations. The cognitive theory of multimedia learning presents the idea that the brain does not interpret a multimedia presentation of words, pictures, and auditory information in a mutually exclusive fashion; rather, these elements are selected and organized dynamically to produce logical mental constructs (Mayer & Moreno, 1998). The cognitive theory of multimedia learning has generated a series of experiments yielding five major principles about how to use multimedia to help students understand what we teach:

1. Students learn better from words and pictures than they do from words alone. In studies, it was found that students who listened to a narration explaining how a bicycle tire pump works—while also viewing a corresponding animation—generated twice as many useful solutions to subsequent problem-solving transfer questions than did students who listened to the same narration without viewing any animation (Mayer & Anderson, 1991, 1992). In another study, students who read a text containing captioned illustrations placed near the corresponding words generated about 65% more useful solutions on a subsequent problem-solving transfer test than did students who simply read the text (Mayer, 1989; Mayer & Gallini, 1990).

2. Students learn better when words and pictures are presented simultaneously rather than successively. Studies showed students had a better understanding of an explanation when corresponding words and pictures were presented at the same time than when they were presented at separate times. One study showed that students who read a document explaining how tire pumps work that included captioned illustrations near the text generated about 75% more useful solutions on problem-solving transfer questions than did students who read the same text with illustrations presented on separate pages (Mayer, 1989; Mayer, Steinhoff, Bower, & Mars, 1995).

3. Words should be presented aurally rather than visually. In a study in which students viewed an animation depicting the formation of lightning—while also listening to a corresponding narration—the authors found that the students generated approximately 50% more useful solutions on a subsequent problem-solving transfer test than did students who viewed the same animation with corresponding on-screen text consisting of the same words as the narration (Mayer & Moreno, 2001). This result is consistent with the cognitive theory of multimedia learning because the on-screen text and animation can overload the visual information processing channel, whereas those students who experienced both aural and visual learning had a more balanced multimedia lesson. Narration is processed in the verbal information processing channel, and animation is processed in the visual information processing channel (Mayer & Moreno, 2001).

4. Students learn better when extraneous material is excluded. When giving a multimedia explanation, use just a few rather than many extraneous words and pictures.

5. Students learn better from a coherent summary that highlights the relevant words and pictures than they do from a longer version of the summary. This principle is also consistent with the cognitive theory of multimedia learning, in which a shorter presentation primes the learner to select relevant information and organize it productively.

Mayer and Gallini (1991) demonstrated that these principles of multimedia use are even more important to follow with students who have less background knowledge and with students who have less effective spatial abilities. Less effective spatial abilities may mean the students will have more difficulty generating their own mental images of the concepts or ideas being taught.

What Does This Theory Mean for Our Teaching?

The short answer to this question is that we need to review each of our old lesson plans to determine how well we are meeting the criteria just outlined and make changes where needed. In this way, we make certain we are optimizing our students' opportunities to learn in our classrooms and online. In addition, we need to develop new lessons that integrate images of all forms into our presentations and explanations. In a 2006 study, Georg Stenberg showed recognition almost doubled for pictures over text. In addition, his findings showed the use of concrete text is more efficient than abstract text because it elicits more visual cues for students (Stenberg, 2006). Figure 8.1 shows only a very small portion of what is an almost endless list of resources for finding images to use in our teaching. A simple search of the term *repositories of images* on the web will yield hundreds of places where free images are available for use. Because images are the easiest thing for our brain to recognize (Zull, 2002), we need to take advantage of these resources in our teaching.

We also need to guide our students to these resources that can greatly aid them in their own learning. For example, a student studying anatomy can find complete and detailed information with extraordinary images at the following sites: Inner Body—Your Guide to Human Anatomy Online, Human-Anatomy.net, and The National Institute of General Medical Sciences—Structures of Life. Perhaps the most extraordinary of all of the resources is the Visible Body, developed by Argosy. It is a comprehensive

FIGURE 8.1
Repositories of Images

- University of Nottingham Image Repository for e-Learning
- SoftChalk CONNECT
- Connexions
- Flickr
- Encyclopedia Britannica
- INTELECOM
- LUNA Commons
- MERLOT
- MIT Visualizing Cultures Project
- Natural Science Digital Library (NSDL)
- The Orange Grove
- WU Academic Commons

human anatomy visualization tool including more than 1,700 anatomical structures. When we facilitate our students' use of resources, we are helping them to take ownership of their learning. Such interactive sites may also pique their curiosity about the subject matter through a sensory experience.

Using Games to Promote Multisensory Learning

One of the messages I have been delivering to faculty members on my campus and around the country for years is that we need to teach the students who are sitting in front of us, not those we wish were sitting in front of us. What I mean by this is that I believe we have an ethical obligation to do the best we can to meet the individual needs of our students, no matter who they are. This includes accepting that they may not be as prepared for college as we would like. However, as all of us barrel into a technological future like a runaway train, it also means that we must figure out how to teach students—who now are plugged in to digital media almost constantly—in ways that meet their learning strengths and preferences.

Don Thompson, Assistant Director of Education and Human Resources at the National Science Foundation, makes this point: "Perhaps the most fatal flaw in the education of young people is that we apprentice young people into 19th century science rather than letting them play 21st century scientist" (Thompson, 2006). According to the Federation of American Scientists, 50% of all Americans and 75% of American heads of household play computer and video games. On average, children ages 8 to 18 spend about 50 minutes per day playing video games. The average adult male spends 7.6 hours per week playing video games, and the average adult female spends 7.4 hours per week (Thompson, 2006). The importance of these data becomes clear when juxtaposed with the learning preferences of digital natives, who prefer:

- Receiving information quickly from multiple multimedia sources
- Parallel processing and multitasking
- Processing pictures, sounds, and video before text
- Random access to hyperlinked multimedia information
- Interacting and networking simultaneously with many others
- Learning "just-in-time"
- Instant gratification and instant rewards
- Learning that is relevant, instantly useful, and fun (Jukes & Dosa, 2003)

Serious Games

There is growing interest in using games as educational tools (Gee, 2003; Prensky, 2001). People are seeing the value of games as models of pedagogically rich, highly motivating learning environments. Commercial games possess many of the elements we look for in learning environments: collaboration, problem solving, higher-order thinking skills, and so on. One new area called serious games is being developed expressly for learning. Serious games fall into two categories: participatory (requiring interactions with other players) and augmented reality (responding to player location) simulation games (Klopfer, 2008). These games are designed for handheld devices and can place learners in real-world contexts that promote transfer of learning from one context to another. They can be produced at much lower cost, using social dynamics and real-world contexts to enhance game play, and can be integrated into the natural flow of instruction much more seamlessly than their big-screen counterparts.

Such games for handheld devices can create compelling and fun educational environments for learners. They are being designed to create activities that are inherently social, authentic, and meaningful; are connected to the real world; are open-ended so they contain multiple pathways; are intrinsically motivating; and are filled with feedback (Klopfer, 2008). Serious games are being used to augment education in K–12, college, health care, military, museums, science, and ecology.

There is evidence that games can support the development of logical thinking and problem solving (Gee, 2003; Whitebread, 1997). Additional studies found that both teachers and parents recognized that game play can support valuable skill development such as strategic thinking, planning, communication, application of numbers, negotiating skills, and group decision making (McFarlane et al., 2002). In Mary Jo Dondlinger's analysis of peer-reviewed material from the last decade that looked at the learning benefits of serious games, she concluded, "There is widespread consensus that games motivate players to spend time on task, mastering the skills a game imparts . . . [A] number of distinct design elements, such as narrative context, rules, goals, rewards, **multisensory cues**, and interactivity, seem necessary to stimulate desired learning outcomes . . . [Serious games] require strategizing, hypothesis testing, or problem-solving, usually with higher order thinking rather than rote memorization or simple comprehension" (Dondlinger, 2007). Our job will be to figure out how to integrate these new tools into our classrooms. The following section discusses a few examples of what is happening in the world of serious games.

Tragedy of the Tuna

The Learning Lab at The Wharton School (www.wharton.upenn.edu) developed Tragedy of the Tuna, a game where students represent a tuna fishing fleet and balance decisions that affect their own group as well as a commonly shared resource.

Customer Service

McDonald's restaurants use serious games to train store personnel in customer service, thanks to 3Dsolve (www.3dsolve.com), the developer of the program.

A Diversity Game for European Students

In this game, players experience the consequences of restraining and promoting cultural diversity. It is a 2D Flash adventure game where the player must solve puzzles and challenges to progress. In the game, the country is at war, and the system encourages you to destroy cultural artifacts from other countries. Players experience the consequences of this destruction and have to fight against the system.

Learning About the Outback in Australia

Serious Games Interactive developed a game that teaches people about the Australian outback and the different animals that inhabit the area in a simple and fun way. The players travel with an aboriginal guide to different locations in Australia and learn important facts about the country while playing fun minigames on the way.

Authentic Learning Is Multisensory

In chapter 3, I made the case for getting our students involved in firsthand learning experiences where they can literally touch and feel as well as see, hear, and/or read what they are learning. Students will recall more from doing the real thing or engaging with an effective simulation than they will from participating in a discussion or speaking on the same topic. Findings showed a 20% greater recall in students who did the real-world activities or engaged in a simulated learning experience (Dale, 1969). An interesting model called augmented learning was designed for creating classrooms and online environments that are more authentic and engage more of students' senses. Developed by Dr. Penny de Byl of the NHTV Breda University of Applied Sciences in the Netherlands, augmented learning is simply the use of artifacts to modify normal teaching and learning situations in an endeavor to immerse and engage students within the learning context. It is a teaching and learning method whereby the real world is adapted with props and contextual information to provide an engrossing and authentic learning environment for students (de Byl, 2009). A fantastic example of this is found at the University of Arizona, where an astronomy class has students create, research, build, and script exhibits for milestones in the Earth's 4.6-billion-year history using Second Life. Although teachers have always been augmenting their learning activities, this simulation creates a tangible experience that captures the essence of *being* in a particular place or context. It enables learners to negotiate meaning based on their own personal cognitive, affective, and kinaesthetic experiences. It assumes learners will construct knowledge through the nonsymbolic, nonreflective, first-person psychological activity that occurs (de Byl, 2009). Once immersed within an augmented world, learners can communicate, investigate, and experiment—either individually or in the company of other learners—to transcend geographical and temporal boundaries. The authentic experiences of these low-risk, nonthreatening environments encourages participation and risk taking. The following are some examples:

- Augmented learning books (where the pages come alive in a virtual world)

- Real-time generation of 3D models from blueprints
- Looking beneath the surface of everyday objects
- Access to live, on demand, location-based information
- Experiencing worlds students might never be able to visit
- Virtually becoming someone or something else (de Byl, 2009)

A vast number of tools are available to immerse our students in what they are learning. If we are to optimize their learning, we will have to investigate these tools and find the ones we can use to help our students learn.

Concept Maps

Mapping is a great multisensory learning tool for teachers and students. Concept maps were developed in 1972 by Joseph Novak of Cornell University. Novak needed a better way to represent children's conceptual understandings of science in a research study he was conducting. What emerged was a visual structure he referred to as a concept map, or a graphical tool used for organizing and representing knowledge. The value of a concept map is that it requires our students to categorize and associate information in a hierarchal way and then translate the information from a narrative form into a visual form, creating a multisensory learning process. One of my colleagues has his students take their chemistry notes from a lecture and map them as a daily assignment. Although the students were not pleased with this extra work, they quickly discovered that they had an enhanced understanding of how the concepts fit together, and it improved recall of their chemistry, as demonstrated by better quiz scores.

The design of a concept map usually includes circles or boxes containing key words representing the concepts, with connections shown by a line linking two concepts. Words on the line linking the two concepts are referred to as linking words or linking phrases, and they specify the relationship between the two concepts (see Figure 8.2 for an example). A concept is labeled most often in a word, although sometimes more than one word or symbols, such as + or %, are used (Novak & Cañas, 2006).

Another characteristic of concept mapping is that the concepts are represented in a hierarchical fashion, with the most inclusive, most general concepts at the top of the map and the more specific, less general concepts arranged below the most general (Novak & Cañas, 2006). Concept maps also contain cross-links, which are relationships or links between concepts in different segments or domains of the concept map (Novak & Cañas, 2006).

FIGURE 8.2
Example of Concept Map With Linking Words

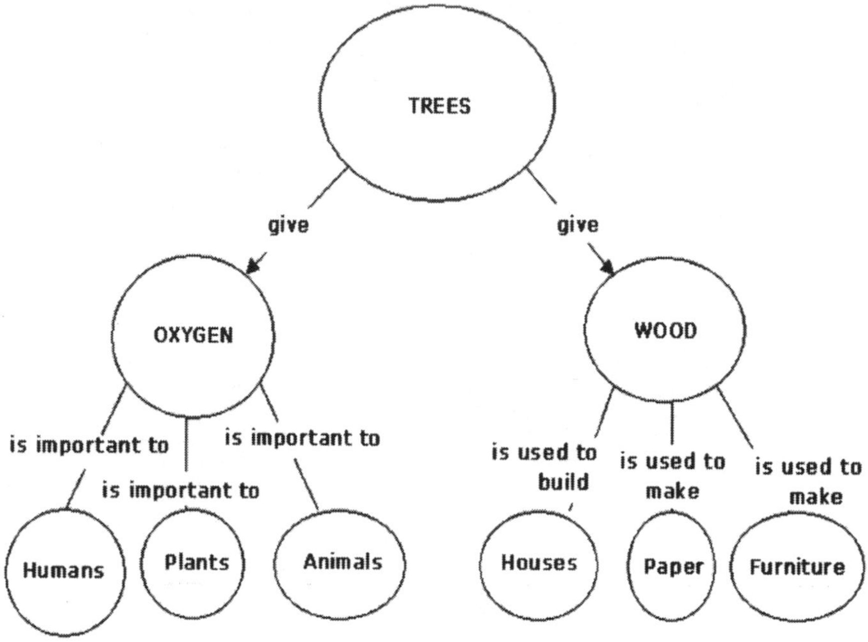

Source: Map by Maria Birbili, 2006.

A well-made concept map grows within a context defined by a focused question or problem. Concept maps are constructed to reflect the organization of the declarative memory system; they facilitate sense making and meaningful learning on the part of individuals who make concept maps (Novak, 1990). They are learning tools, but they can also be effective evaluation tools. Students can be encouraged to use the maps to discover the patterns in their learning and in the content we teach them (Mintzes et al., 2000; Novak, 1990; Novak & Gowin, 1984). Concept maps are also effective in identifying both valid and invalid ideas held by students and for identifying the relevant knowledge a learner possesses before or after instruction (Edwards & Fraser, 1983). Concept mapping can also promote metacognitive awareness by making knowledge explicit. Students can see what they know, what is missing, and whether the connections they are making between ideas are correct (McAleese, 1994).

How to Use Concept Maps

The beauty of a concept map is that it has many possible applications that can enhance teaching and students' learning. The following are several examples of its use:

1. Organizing information to be used in solving a problem
2. Making a visual display of a narrative story line
3. Classifying the characteristics of person, place, or item
4. Developing a prewriting outline
5. Arranging the concepts of an entire textbook chapter in a visual display
6. Designing a persuasive argument for a paper
7. Presenting the similarities and differences in objects or ideas
8. Showing cause-and-effect processes
9. Creating a diagram of the day's lesson plan
10. Assessing student learning
11. Mapping class notes

When students map a textbook chapter, for example, they can see how the entire chapter is connected before beginning their reading, and should lead to improved comprehension. You can use the concept maps that students create for feedback about their understanding of concepts or ideas.

Planning Is the Key

As is true with all aspects of learner-centered practice, multisensory learning activities require time spent in planning. We will need to consider how to integrate multisensory practices into our instruction *and* how to get our students to use their senses in the learning they do outside class. Many of us do not have a lot of practice in thinking about how to use all of the senses in our teaching. However, moving toward a multisensory approach is an important step in enhancing our students' opportunities to learn.

9

PATTERNS

A Major Element in Effective Teaching and Learning

Human cognitive process involves actively creating linkages among concepts, skill elements,
people, and experiences. For the individual
learner, this will be about making meaning by
establishing and reworking patterns, relationships, and connections. New biological research reveals that connection-making is
the core of both mental activity and brain
development.

(Ewell, 1997, p. 7)

P atterns are everywhere. Charles Darwin saw patterns in the various
life forms he observed on his travels, which later led him to formulate
his evolutionary theory. Gregor Mendel observed the patterns of
inheritance of pea plant traits and, as a result, provided us our first understanding of heredity. When I was learning to play baseball, my coach always
talked about watching the opposing pitcher to see how often he threw a
fastball and when he would throw something slower. He wanted us to recognize a pattern so when it was our turn to bat, we might have an advantage
by knowing when the pitcher might throw a slow one that we could hit. Or
maybe he told me this advice only because he knew I couldn't hit the fastball.
Regardless, teaching our students to be observant, to look for the patterns
that exist in all knowledge and specifically their course material, is one of the
most important lifelong learning skills we can help them develop.

To view chapter-related videos please go to tinyurl.com/learnercenteredvideo.

Patterned Learning

Because volumes have been written about how the human brain uses patterns, I realized I needed to zero-in on just a couple of key elements of patterning that would best help all of us optimize our students' learning. The first of these elements is to help students discover the patterns that exist within our own content areas. We must build into our courses activities and demonstrations that reveal how our course material is ordered and organized so students can better see how the course knowledge is interconnected. Equally important is to demonstrate the thinking patterns used most often in our content areas. For example, how does one think like a historian or a sociologist? These crucial instructional elements can help our students gain a deeper understanding of our course material rather than seeing it as a set of disconnected pieces one memorizes for a test. The second element in using patterning is to assist our students in learning how to use patterning processes such as similarity and difference, comparison and contrast, cause and effect, and many other relational methods to enhance their learning and memory. Many of our students have adopted very simple systems of organizing their information. These simple systems are less than ideal for promoting understanding and recall.

Our Brains Seek Patterns

Harvard psychiatrist John Ratey, in his book *A User's Guide to the Brain*, described the human brain "as a pattern seeking device" (Ratey, 2001). He wrote, "The brain works by relating whole concepts to one another and looks for similarities, differences and relationships between them" (Ratey, 2001, p. 5). We see the importance of patterns every day, for example, when we read about a medical researcher who noticed a pattern in data that then led to the development of a cure for a disease. We hear about researchers in economics who saw patterns in consumer spending, leading to new marketing strategies or product development. Patterns are a major key to successful learning.

The human cognitive process involves actively creating linkages among concepts, skill elements, people, and experiences in order to make meaning by establishing and reworking patterns, relationships, and connections (Ewell, 1997). Our brain patterns constantly change. Every time we learn something new, we create additional patterns and alter some previously established patterns. Patterns are so much a part of how our brains work that when we feel like we don't have command of our lives, our brains often invent patterns that offer a sense of self-control (Whitson & Galinsky, 2008).

In a learner-centered classroom, the patterns we need to focus on are the patterns that represent the meaningful organization and categorization of the information in our subjects (Caine & Caine, 1991). These patterns are what we instantly recognize and use all the time to do our research and teaching, but somehow we fail to share them with our students. The failure is likely the result of these patterns becoming so familiar to us that we just assume our students must see them as clearly as we do.

Conditioned to a Linear World

Our students have spent most of their K–12 experiences engaged in linear learning activities, where the learning is organized in basic forms of space, time, or process (Barrett, 1991). When our students are faced with information that does not follow these basic structures, it can be trying. For example, in the social sciences, entire courses are taught around a single major pivot concept or topic, like the study of the family, where multiple issues, factors, and people affect this pivotal concept in multiple ways. Often, these multiple ways do not follow any predetermined path our students can recognize easily, making the learning more challenging or even frustrating. Recognizing the patterns of our subject matter unlocks the secret of examining, exploring, and understanding the material rather than just scratching the surface of it.

This concept can be illustrated by the learning of chess. If I learn only the surface of the game, the names of the pieces, how each piece moves, and the rules, I can play a game of chess. I don't really know anything about how chess is played, however, because I don't recognize the patterns within the game that would tell me what moves to make or not make. I can play, but I don't have any way of improving my game. Adrian de Groot, the Dutch chess master and psychologist, wrote about how master chess players use patterns. Their unique talents, he wrote, are related to their ability to make meaningful connections between the current chessboard configurations and both previous and future chessboard configurations. They can do this because they have studied the patterns of tens of thousands of games and can recall as many as 50,000 or more chess board configurations. He writes that improvement comes only from learning more and more meaningful patterns (de Groot, 1946).

Learner-Centered Teaching Is About Teaching Patterns

Learner-centered teaching (LCT) is about helping our students to learn that there are patterns in all knowledge and that their job is to look for them constantly. By pointing out the patterns of our subjects and showing students how these patterns can help them to understand and recall the course information, we are optimizing their opportunities for learning. In my Education (EDUC) 440 course, "Reading in the Content Areas," I had future teachers from both the sciences and the arts in the same class. I found that those students from the sciences, who had spent a great deal of time learning the patterns of synthesis thinking that are absolutely crucial to successful science learning, struggled when I asked them to develop analysis questions for the sample reading assignments. I also found that my arts students had similar problems with developing synthesis questions because the bulk of their training had been in analysis of written and spoken language. Each group simply hadn't been exposed to the patterns of thinking outside their concentration areas and thus struggled. Once I gave them some help in recognizing how synthesis and analysis questions are organized and structured, they improved immediately. They simply didn't know the pattern or at least hadn't used it very often.

Helping Students to Use Their Own Patterns

Our students need help in recognizing their own personal patterns of information organization. This may sound strange, but when I asked faculty groups to describe how their students organize their course information to maximize learning and recall the information clearly later, the following were the four most common answers:

1. They don't—at least not very well.
2. In outline form.
3. Exactly the same way I teach it.
4. They use note cards.

Although our students have developed excellent abilities to recognize patterns in many aspects of their lives, they often do not transfer them to the classroom. Perhaps 12 or more years in a teacher-centered environment, where they were asked to memorize information, is the cause. Education should be about increasing the patterns that students can use, recognize, and communicate. As the ability to see and work with patterns expands, our students get smarter (Caine, McClintic, & Klimek, 2009).

We can help our students to understand that making sense of something is not the same as memorizing it. For example, one of the most effective ways to help students make meaning of their course content and improve recall of the content is called recoding. Recoding is the process by which a student translates the academic course information into her or his own words (Deno & Markell, 2001). Students can do this by giving an example or metaphor, or just by explaining it in their own way. The key is that the students' own words are their most familiar pattern. How they structure their language and the kind of language they use will be very familiar to them and likely easier to recall. If students can't translate new learning into their own words, it is a very good indicator that they have not made meaning of the information and need additional assistance.

The first skill I teach in my reading improvement courses is annotation, which is a form of recoding. I want my students to learn to use their own word patterns to identify the important information in their text because it will be easier for them to recall the information and to let me know if they comprehend it. This is simply getting students to use the patterns they are most familiar with to their best learning advantage. I also teach it first because it is an attention-focusing skill, and lack of attention is often one of my students' reading weaknesses. It is not possible to annotate if you don't pay attention and comprehend what you read.

When Students Don't Recognize the Patterns

A lack of pattern recognition can cause students to treat information as if it doesn't even exist because they don't recognize the information as being meaningful. Take our chess example from earlier. If a novice chess player sees the board but cannot recognize the significance of the pieces' location, their location cannot help her make her next move. This is why it is so important to reveal the patterns of our course content to our students and, if at all possible, draw connections between the content's patterns and patterns that are familiar to our students. The human brain searches for meaning by attempting to discern and understand patterns as they occur (Caine, McClintic, & Klimek, 2009, p. 89). Failure to see patterns equates to a lack of meaningful learning.

Use These Examples to Help Your Students See Patterns

The following exercises can help your students to understand the value of looking for patterns and the need to use patterning processes in their own learning. Place the following set of numbers on a PowerPoint slide (or another medium that all students can see): 13276796753. On the next slide, place the same 11 numbers, but organize them into the familiar pattern of a phone number: 1(327)679-6753. Show the students the first slide with "13276796753" and then the second, and ask them which slide would be easier to learn and remember. The choice is always the second slide. Students indicate that the information on the second slide has been chunked, thus making it appear as four pieces of information rather than eleven. Because the 11 numbers on the second slide are now in the meaningful pattern of a phone number, which students not only recognize but have used thousands of times, the numbers on the second slide are much easier to learn and remember. It is important to point out that each slide contained the same 11 numbers but by using the power of patterning, the somewhat meaningless information on the first slide has been made more meaningful.

Here is another example. As indicated earlier, the brain is a pattern-seeking device (Ratey, 2001, p. 5) and will work to find an existing pattern, even if it doesn't recognize any pattern in the information at first. Show the slide in Figure 9.1 to your students and ask them to raise their hands when they recognize the pattern that exists within the information.

Most students need only 3 to 10 seconds to find the pattern: "NRA NBC MTV FBI CBS." I use this demonstration to explain that our brains

FIGURE 9.1

NRANBCMTVFBICBS

will keep looking to find a pattern that will bring meaning to the information. It is not necessary to feel dismay if you don't initially understand what is being taught in a class. We all need to trust that our brains will keep working to find the meaningful pattern, even while we sleep (Ribeiro, 2004).

Students Find Different Patterns

Figure 9.2 shows another activity that I give to my students to get them thinking about how to look for meaningful patterns to help learning and recall. The activity is simple. I ask the students to organize all of the words in the exercise into patterns that would make them most easy to learn and remember. I tell them there is no right or wrong pattern and they can choose whatever patterns they find most meaningful. It is very interesting to see how many different patterns students find to organize the information, and how some students create patterns that are much more meaningful, and therefore easier to recall, than others. At first, many students begin organizing the words into categories such as fruits, vegetables, meats, and dairy products. Others start making alphabetical lists, for example, putting all the words beginning with C in the same category. These patterns clearly make sense and are not bad choices. Some students create categories such as fatty foods and healthy foods; foods that go in a salad; foods you serve at each course of a dinner; or breakfast, lunch, and dinner foods. These patterns are more meaningful because the words are connected in ways we actually use them. They are not isolated bits of information. This activity showed students how finding more meaningful patterns makes learning and recall easier and that some patterns are more useful than others.

FIGURE 9.2
Find the Patterns

eggs steak	spinach	turkey	strawberries	cream	cheese
peas	celery	butter	lettuce milk	ham	cream cheese
pork	oranges	tangerines	buttermilk bacon	olives	
plums	apples	donuts	cookies bananas	fish	
cherries	brownies mangos	lemons	cookies	cream puffs greens	
okra	blueberries carrots	ice cream	broccoli	potatoes	
chicken duck cauliflower	rice	toast	grapefruit		

Examples to Use in Explaining Patterns

Periodic Table of Elements

How did the periodic table come to be organized the way that it is? It took recognition of certain patterns of behavior and structure of the elements. Scientists knew there had to be commonalities and differences in the elements and looked for these patterns. At first, the table was organized by atomic weight. Although this was a fairly accurate organization, it was later discovered that some elements didn't fit this pattern. It was then organized by atomic number, which represents the number of protons contained in the nucleus of that element. Additional patterns were recognized, which led to future organization of the table into periods (horizontal rows), groups (vertical columns), and trends (metals, nonmetals, and metalloids). Why the chemistry lesson? The pattern of the periodic table—how it is organized and why it is organized in this way—must be understood if the students are to use the table successfully and understand chemistry. Just memorizing the elements in their places on the table will not help students to learn chemistry (Devlin, 2002, p. 12).

Movie Patterns

I have listed here the top ten patterns for today's movies:

Horror Movie with the Psycho Killer	Buddy Cop Movie
Action Movie	Romance
The Twist	Stereotype Shakeup
Epic War Movie	Teen Comedy
Outrageous Comedy	The Underdog

Ask your students to tell you what usually happens in each of these types of movies. What they will tell you is the patterns of the movies' development and conclusion. It is an easy exercise to get students thinking about predictable patterns, which they can translate to their course content. It also helps them to look for those patterns and then use them to aid their understanding and recall, which are powerful tools for learning.

Revealing the Patterns of Our Content

This cognitive process involves actively creating linkages among concepts, skill elements, people, and experiences. For the individual learner, this will be about making meaning by establishing and reworking patterns, relationships, and connections. New biological research reveals that making connections is the core of both mental activity and brain development (Ewell, 1997). As our students strive to make meaning by reworking the patterns of our content areas, we need to assist them by making these patterns more visible.

How is your history, humanities, or biology course organized? How do the various content materials connect? What patterns are common and repeat in your course material? How can you teach students to recognize these patterns? What prior knowledge of the content patterns do you expect learners to have when they begin the course? What kinds of thinking patterns are common in people who know and use this content? These are many of the questions we need to be asking ourselves as we plan our course lessons. It is not enough to know and love our content. If we are to optimize our students' learning, we need to connect the patterns of our content areas to the patterns of our students' prior knowledge. The first step is to outline how the course content is organized as a subject area. The next step is to define which patterns we will use in presenting this information to our students. This decision is influenced by the answers to the following three questions:

1. What patterns are we familiar with and comfortable in using when teaching this subject? It is important to note that we might have to alter these patterns if, during our planning, we discover other patterns that would clearly optimize students' learning.
2. What resources are available to us to present the information in these chosen patterns? For example, do you have ready access to the Internet, classroom projection systems, computer information systems, and any other learning media needed?
3. What patterns are our students most familiar with in their learning? Which of these patterns also fits with our subject matter and instructional decisions?

The process of integrating meaningful patterns into our teaching is not difficult. Most of us already do this without thinking about it. The change that is needed is to make the patterns overt by making certain that our students recognize the patterns and use them to expand their critical thinking skills, develop deeper understanding of course content, and improve recall of the course material. For example, if the course material is very linear, we probably use a time line, sequence of major events, or significant people as organizational pillars. Making certain that our students understand why we do this and how this pattern helps a learner to comprehend the material optimizes our students' learning. There is no absolute right or wrong way, just the way that best connects with the students and helps them to both understand and remember.

Instructional Patterns

Cognitive science research has helped develop instructional practices that have been shown to enhance student learning. These approaches often require using repeating patterns of instruction to promote long-term learning. I have included the following two approaches as examples of how patterning fits into our instructional decisions.

1. Interleave demonstrated example solutions and problem-solving exercises. When teaching mathematical or science problem solving, teachers should interleave demonstrated example solutions and problem-solving exercises, alternating between worked examples, demonstrating one possible solution path, and problems that each student is asked to solve for himself or herself. Research has shown that this interleaving markedly enhances student learning (Institute of Education Sciences, 2007). By solving their own problems between the demonstrated examples, students are motivated to pay more attention to the demonstrated examples because they help them prepare for the next problem and/or resolve a question from the past problem. Also, having problems to solve helps students recognize what they do not understand (Institute of Education Sciences, 2007, p.16).

2. Connect and integrate abstract and concrete representations of concepts. One of the most difficult things to teach well is abstract concepts. Cognitive research suggests that we need to connect and integrate abstract representations of a concept with concrete representations of the same concept. This pattern of connecting different forms of representations helps students master the concept being taught, and it improves the likelihood that students will use it appropriately across a range of different contexts (Bottge, Rueda, Serlin, Hung, & Kwon, 2007). An abstract idea, like a mathematical function, can be expressed in many different ways: concisely in mathematical symbols like "$y = 2x$"; visually in a line graph that starts at 0 and goes by 2 units for every 1 unit up the line; discretely in a table

showing that 0 goes to 0, 1 goes to 2, 2 goes to 4, and so on; practically, in a real-world scenario like making $2 for every mile you walk in a walkathon; and physically, by walking at 2 miles per hour (Pashler, Bain, Bottge, Graesser, Koedinger, McDaniel, & Metcalfe, 2007, p. 16).

It is also important to recognize that when students first encounter a new idea, they may pick up on the wrong features of the examples we give them. For instance, they might think that averages are about sports if we give them mostly sports examples. A variety of representations and explicit discussion of the connections between them are needed to avoid having students develop misconceptions (Pashler et al., 2007, p. 17).

Patterns That Students Use Most

When I began my work as a faculty developer, one of the first things I did was attend a teaching conference for K–12 educators. I went hoping I would improve my understanding of what went into effective lesson planning. I wanted to understand better the planning process these teachers used to help them connect to their students' prior knowledge. I knew my K–12 colleagues were much more concerned about their students' background knowledge than my colleagues in higher education were. What I discovered is that these K–12 teachers were all about patterns. They didn't use that exact word, but as they described their planning processes, I realized that their goals were to organize their material in ways that their students could easily recognize and to teach their students how to organize their new learning in ways that would be easier to understand and recall. The planning process was all about finding the right patterns.

How students organize knowledge influences how they learn and apply what they know. Students naturally make connections between and among pieces of knowledge. When those connections form knowledge structures that are accurately and meaningfully organized, students are better able to retrieve and apply their knowledge effectively and efficiently. In contrast, when knowledge is connected in inaccurate or random ways, students can fail to retrieve or apply it appropriately (Carnegie Mellon Learning Principles, 2011).

Similarity and Difference; Comparison and Contrast

If we could pick only one pattern with which to teach our subject and give our students only one pattern to help them learn, it would likely be that of similarity and difference. It is perhaps the pattern used most often in all of teaching and learning. It is kind of a universal default pattern. Two hundred thousand years ago, it was important for our ancestors to notice the similarities and differences between animals they hunted and those that hunted them in order to eat and to remain safe. Our students have been using this pattern even before they began preschool. For example, when we ask our students to study the characteristics of different organisms, we are asking them to find patterns of similarity and difference. This type of pattern helps them begin to understand how things are related. Such patterns may be useful in sorting and classifying different living things: flowers with five petals, animals with hooves, amphibians with a tail, and so on. When we look at a group of organisms, all bees, for example, we find that we can learn more about the individual species when we examine how members of that species are alike and different from other species.

We have been engaging our students in the process of comparing and contrasting two items, ideas, authors, and so on as a way to help them understand individual differences and distinctions between information since we introduced content to them in elementary school. When students practice sorting and classifying living things and then describe why an organism belongs in a certain group, they are using these common patterns to enhance their understanding and recall. Whether we are comparing authors' styles or periods of art or Civil War strategies, our students know how to proceed in the learning process when they are asked to find the similarities and differences or compare and contrast sets of information.

Cause and Effect

What were the causes of the U.S. Civil War, the Vietnam War, or the recent great recession in the United States? What are the causes of the AIDS epidemic or the Black Plague? What are the causes of unrest in the Middle East? What effects can be attributed to phenomena such as global warming or the counterculture movement of the 1960s? What were the effects of the civil rights movement of the 1950s and 1960s, Hurricane Katrina in New Orleans and the Delta region of the South, or the H1N1 flu scare? Our students have been asked to explore the causes and effects of events throughout their K–12 experience. I recall being asked by Sister Mary what caused the fight on the playground in fourth grade. I also recall the effects of fighting in fourth grade when I had to write "I must not fight on the playground" 500 times. Cause-and-effect papers are among the most common in any composition course. It is a pattern our students know well but often not deeply. It is not uncommon to find that our students know only the surface reasons why something happened. Ask them what causes AIDS, and they may say sexual contact or blood exchanges, but they likely won't know that the disease is caused by a retrovirus that multiplies in the human immune system's CD4 + T cells and kills vast numbers of the cells it infects. The result is disease symptoms (E-Health MD, 2011). Using the pattern of cause and effect allows for deeper exploration of ideas and events and requires more critical thinking than just sorting information into categories. We need to help our students recognize the kind of time, resources, and intellectual energy that can go into finding a cause. For a scientist to say that she has found the cause of something, we know that she has explored all of the possible causes and eliminated all possible causes except one. This process requires much deeper thought than just categorizing information with similar or different features. Using cause and effect in teaching is a great construct for getting our students to do more critical thinking and less surface learning. It is also a great way to help them recognize the complexity of knowledge and the complexities of their own lives.

Other Patterns Students Commonly Use

In addition to similarity and difference, and cause and effect, our students have spent a great deal of time using each of the following organizational structures in their learning:

1. **Hierarchy.** Our students are very familiar with information organized in order of importance from best to worst, biggest to smallest, newest to oldest, and so on. Flow charts, outlines, and cognitive maps are common ways that students have used hierarchy to aid their learning.
2. **Alphabetical order.** From the time our students entered preschool, they have been exposed to the pattern of alphabetical order. Just ask anyone whose name begins with an A or a Z. Do a search of organizing by alphabetical order and you will find websites that will do it for you. Just put in your information and hit the button. This pattern does not enhance understanding of the information or show meaningful relationships between or among pieces of information. But it is so familiar that, as a beginning point for learning new terms or vocabulary words, it may help our students to get started.

3. **Their own language.** Earlier in the chapter, I mentioned how I teach my students to annotate their text material as a way to improve their recall and check their comprehension. The key element at work in annotation is that the words used are the students' own. The most familiar pattern for our students is their own language. The specific ways in which they use their language, order it, personalize it, and abbreviate it create patterns that are easier for them to recognize and recall.

Patterns and Learner-Centered Teaching

As I have written many times in this book, our goal is to optimize our students' opportunities to learn. I knew that I had taken a positive step forward in optimizing their learning when I had included a focus on helping students discover the patterns within their assigned reading materials and taught them how to take the material and place it into meaningful patterns that would aid recall. Like many other aspects of learner-centered teaching, the lesson planning makes the difference in what learning takes place. As we assist our students in recognizing the patterns of our course material and help them to see the importance of using patterns in their learning, we become more learner-centered in our teaching.

REPETITION AND ELABORATION

Your brain is doing work for you even when you're resting.

(Davachi, 2010)

Two older gentlemen, Bob and Sid, decided to meet at the golf course one sunny Tuesday to play a round of golf. Bob, who had very poor eyesight, asked Sid if he'd watch to see where his shots went. With a congenial grin, Sid said he'd be happy to. Bob swung his club and proceeded to hit his first ball. He turned to Sid and asked, "Did you see it?" Sid replied, "Yes. Yes, I did." Bob asked, "Well, then, where did it go?" Sid shook his head and said, "You asked me to watch where it went and I did. Now, remembering where it went, that's a whole other story!"

In this tale, Sid likely has some very valid reasons about why he has trouble recalling something that just happened, and those reasons likely include advanced age and possibly disease. With few exceptions, age and disease are not the reasons our students can't recall what we taught them the day or sometimes just an hour before. The causes of these memory failures have much more to do with how the information was inputted by the students, what they did immediately after the class ended, and what they did with the information in the days and weeks following their initial interaction with it.

This chapter explores the current research on what helps and hinders the recall of information in a college learning environment. It also suggests instructional tools we can use to help our students retain information in long-term memory. Finally, the chapter discusses study practices our students can use to enhance their recall of the important information they need for academic success.

To view chapter-related videos please go to tinyurl.com/learnercenteredvideo.

What Do We Know About Human Memory?

Memory is one of the most researched areas in all of science. The search for how the brain organizes memories and where those memories are acquired and stored has been a never-ending quest among brain researchers for decades. Researchers from biology, neuroscience, psychology, and related areas all have an interest in understanding how the human brain forms, keeps, and loses memories. Although scientists haven't figured out exactly how the system works, there is enough information to make some educated guesses (Mohs, 2010).

To encode a memory properly, people must first be paying attention (Duclukovic & Wagner, 2006). Because they can't pay attention to everything all the time, most of what they encounter every day is simply filtered out, and only a few stimuli pass into their conscious awareness. What scientists do not know is whether stimuli are screened out during the sensory input stage or only after the brain processes its significance. What scientists do know is that how people, including our students, pay attention to information may be the most important factor in how much of it they actually recall (Mohs, 2010).

The Brain and Memory Formation

Encoding is the first step in creating a memory. It is a biological phenomenon, rooted in the senses, that begins with perception. Each new but separate sensation travels to the part of our brain called the hippocampus, which integrates these perceptions as they are occurring into one single experience. Experts believe that the hippocampus, along with the frontal cortex, is responsible for analyzing various sensory inputs and deciding if they are worth remembering. If they are, they may become part of our long-term memory (Mohs, 2010; Smith & Squire, 2009).

New neuron connections are made, and they change all the time. Brain cells work together in a network, organizing themselves into groups that specialize in different kinds of information processing. As one brain cell sends signals to another, the synapse between the two gets stronger. The more signals sent between them, the stronger the connection grows. Thus, with each new experience, your brain slightly rewires its physical structure. In fact, how you use your brain helps determine how your brain is organized. Scientists call this flexibility of the brain plasticity (Mohs, 2010).

As our students learn and experience the world, more connections in their brains are created. Their brains organize and reorganize in response to their learning experiences, forming memories triggered by their experiences, education, and/or training (Diekelmann & Born, 2010). These new networks are reinforced with use so that, as our students learn and practice new information, intricate circuits of knowledge and memory are built in their brains.

Sleep and Memory

Memory researchers have suspected for some time that sleep plays a powerful role in the consolidation of long-term memories. Recent findings confirm these suspicions. Sleep has been identified as a state that optimizes the consolidation of newly acquired information in memory, depending on the specific conditions of learning and the timing of sleep. Consolidation during sleep promotes both quantitative and qualitative changes of memory representations (Diekelmann & Born, 2010). A Duke University study found periods of slow-wave sleep produce a recall, and probably amplification, of memory traces. Ensuing episodes of REM sleep trigger the expression of genes to store what was processed during slow-wave sleep (Ribeiro et al., 2004). A study conducted at the Beth Israel Deaconess Medical Center using MRI scans showed brain regions shift dramatically during sleep: "When you're asleep, it seems as though you are shifting memory to more efficient storage regions within the brain. Consequently, when you awaken, memory tasks can be performed both more quickly and accurately and with less stress and anxiety" (Walker, 2009).

The implications of these findings for our students are significant. If they don't get a reasonable amount of sleep (7 to 8 hours), they are not giving their brains enough time to take the day's new information, consolidate it, and start the process of making it a more permanent memory. I regularly survey my students (about 100 each semester) about the number of hours of sleep they get on average. The range is usually from 3 to 10 hours a night, with the vast majority getting less than 7. There is nothing scientific about this survey, but the results are always dismaying. It is clear that our students cannot optimize their learning without getting enough sleep.

It is also important to note that many studies over the past decade suggest people who take a nap after learning a new task remember it better than those who don't (Walker, 2009). One NASA study showed astronauts who napped 20 to 30 minutes had a 37% improvement in cognitive functioning following the nap over astronauts who did not nap (Medina, 2008).

Forgetting

One of the leading memory researchers in the world, psychologist Elizabeth Loftus from the University of California at Irvine, has identified four major reasons why people forget: retrieval failure, interference, failure to store, and motivated forgetting. The first three—retrieval failures, interference, and failure to store—have significant importance for helping us understand why our students may forget the information and skills we thought we taught them so effectively (as cited in Cherry, 2010).

1. Retrieval Failure

One common cause of forgetting is simply an inability to retrieve a memory. One possible explanation is known as decay theory. Decay theory suggests that, over time, memory traces begin to fade and disappear. If information is not retrieved and rehearsed, it will eventually be lost. One problem with this theory is that researchers don't know whether the failure to recall something means it is no longer in our memory or there is another reason why it can't be retrieved (Brown, 1958; McKone, 1998).

2. Interference

Another theory known as interference theory suggests that some memories compete and interfere with other memories. When information is very similar to other information that was previously stored in memory, interference is more likely to occur. For example, a student studying both physics and chemistry may confuse the problem process used in one or the other subject because the math involved in both is very similar. There are two basic types of interference:

- **Proactive interference** occurs when an old memory makes it more difficult or impossible to remember a new memory.
- **Retroactive interference** occurs when new information interferes with your ability to remember previously learned information (Underwood & Postman, 1960).

3. Failure to Store

We also forget information because it never actually made it into long-term memory. Encoding failures sometimes prevent information from entering long-term memory. A student might not pay attention to the information carefully enough to record it accurately, missing important details. Obviously, if this information is not recorded, there is nothing to be stored (Ebbinghaus, 1885; Rinck, 1999).

4. Motivated Forgetting

Sometimes, we may actively work to forget memories, especially those of traumatic or disturbing events or experiences. The two basic forms of motivated forgetting are suppression, a conscious form of forgetting, and repression, an unconscious form of forgetting (psychologists are unclear about repression because it is almost impossible to study). In Harvard psychologist Daniel Schacter's 2001 book, *Seven Sins of Memory,* he suggests three basic reasons why college students forget:

Blocking: Information is stored but cannot be accessed (Schacter, 2001). The classic case of this is test anxiety, where clearly the student has studied and knows the information, but the anxiety of the test environment interferes with the recall of the information (Cassady & Johnson, 2002).

Misattribution: A memory is attributed to the wrong situation or source (Schacter & Dodson, 2001). This happens when students take several similar courses, often in their major areas of study. The information is so similar it becomes difficult to determine which course, class, or text it came from.

Transience: Memory is lost over time (Schacter, 2001). Sixty-five percent of a lecture is lost in the first hour (Medina, 2008). Transience exists for both short- and long-term memory. In a 2009 study, Davachi and Staresina suggested that, if you do not allow yourself a break after learning something new, it is costly to your learning. Students may be hindering their brain's ability to consolidate memories and experiences by taking classes back to back. From the brain scans, researchers could tell that daydreaming during the rest period improved the participants' recall (Staresina & Davachi, 2009). Subjects who took rest periods showed a greater magnitude of connection-making activity in their brains and were better able to recall face–object picture pairs. These findings show that certain kinds of brain activity actually increase during waking rest and are correlated with better memory consolidation. "Taking a rest may actually contribute to your success at work or school" (Davachi & Staresina, 2009).

Stress and Memory—A New Finding

Creating a safe learning environment that is engaging, interesting, and challenging is more important than ever given new findings about the role that stress plays in inhibiting learning and memory. It has been known that severe stress lasting weeks or months can impair cell communication in the brain's learning and memory region, but a new study by Dr. Tallie Z. Baram, the Danette Shepard Chair in Neurological Sciences in the University of California Irvine School of Medicine, provides the first evidence that short-term stress has the same effect. The study found that, rather than involving the widely known stress hormone cortisol, which circulates throughout the body, acute stress activated selective molecules called corticotropin releasing hormones (CRH), which disrupted the process by which the brain collects and stores memories. The release of CRH in the hippocampus, the brain's primary learning and memory center, led to the rapid disintegration of the cells' dendritic spines, which in turn limited the ability of synapses to collect and store memories (Baram, Chen, Dubé, & Rice, 2008). It is unlikely we will ever teach students who are totally free of stress. But we can work toward providing learning environments that reduce their stress and engage them so they will focus on the learning and forget the stress, at least while they are in our classes.

Enhancing Memory—Research Findings

Almost daily, new findings reveal an increased understanding of the learning and memory processes of the human brain. I believe it is our responsibility as professionals to do our best to stay informed and, when appropriate, try to integrate research-based changes into our teaching. This is no easy task because the pace of research is extraordinary. The findings I have included in this chapter were chosen because they may have significant impact on learning and memory in the next several years.

So much is written about the problems people have with memory that when research suggests real ways to boost memory, it is a refreshing surprise. One such study found that the combination of caffeine and sugar (glucose) enhanced attention, learning, and memory. The conclusions suggested that a combination of caffeine and glucose has beneficial effects on attention (sequential reaction-time tasks) and learning and also on the consolidation of verbal memory; none of these effects were observed when the substances were consumed separately (Serra-Grabulosa, Adan, Falcón, & Bargalló, 2010). The study's main finding was that the combination of the two substances improves cognitive performance in terms of sustained attention and working memory by increasing the efficiency of the areas of the brain responsible for these two functions. There appears to be a definite synergistic effect between the two substances in which one boosts the effect of the other (Serra-Grabulosa et al., 2010).

Much is known about the neural processes that occur during learning, but until now it has not been clear why it occurs during certain brain states and not others. Now researchers have been able to study, in isolation, the specific neurotransmitter that enhances learning and memory. Acetylcholine is released in the brain during learning and is critical for the acquisition of new memories. Its role is to facilitate the activity of *N*-methyl *D*-aspartate (NMDA) receptors, proteins that control the strength of connections between nerve cells in the brain. The discovery opens new opportunities for boosting cognitive function in the face of diseases such as Alzheimer's, as well as new ways of enhancing memory in healthy people (Isaac, Buchanan, Muller, & Mellor, 2009).

The Very Near Future—Drugs to Enhance Memory

Steven Ferris, executive director of the Silberstein Aging and Dementia Research Center at New York University School of Medicine, says that just around the corner looms a new world where people of all ages could reach for a pill that would strengthen the brain, enabling it to learn faster and make the lessons last. Scientists have learned so much about the way the human brain learns and remembers that they are fashioning the first generation of memory enhancers (Ferris, 2003). Amy F.T. Arnsten, professor of neurobiology and psychology at Yale University, cautions that many neuroscientists and pharmaceutical companies assume that the brain is homogeneous. She says that we have to respect the vast chemical differences between brains and learn how to target these drugs intelligently (Arnstern et al., 2010).

Teaching for Long-Term Recall

The question I ask every group of faculty members I work with is, What information in your course would make you happy that your students still knew it a year after they completed your class? I suggest that the answer to this question should define our course learning outcomes. Why bother teaching skills and information if we don't care whether it is learned? I also ask this question as a way to begin a discussion about how to teach in ways that promote our students knowing the skills and information we want them to know a year or more after the course has ended. I call this teaching for long-term recall.

The key elements in developing long-term memories are the repetition and elaboration of the information and skills being taught. Higher education is often the place where faculty members speak about "covering" the content rather than helping students to develop long-term memories for the content. In a learner-centered teaching (LCT) environment, the goal is learning that can be used, transferred, and recalled months and years later. What follows are several suggestions about how to teach for long-term recall. None of the suggestions require significant changes in our teaching approach or a great deal of additional work. What they do require is focusing on just what we want the students to learn and nothing else.

1. **Teach students to space their practice.** Spacing the study of material has powerful (and typically nonmonotonic) effects on retention, with optimal memory occurring when spacing is some modest fraction of the final retention interval (perhaps about 10% to 20%). Longer than optimal spacing is not nearly as harmful to final memory as shorter than optimal spacing (Pashler, Rohrer, Cepeda, & Carpenter, 2007). This research confirms what many of us have known: Short, intensive study (cramming) does not lead to long-term recall. What is new in these findings, however, is that there is optimal spacing between study or review activities to promote the best recall, and that time period equals 10% to 20% of the time between the initial learning and the test. If the test is four weeks away (28 days), studying or reviewing every 3 to 4 days would be best. Because faculty members teach course material in intensive time frames, it is not always possible for students to use the study spacing recommended in this research.

2. **Cumulative tests or exams.** I have mentioned this earlier in the book. It is such an easy way to force students to repeat, relearn, and elaborate their course content that I wanted to repeat myself. We simply need to determine the one, two, three, or more most important elements that we want our students to understand deeply and be able to recall, and retest these elements throughout the semester. In addition to the repetition and relearning, which leads to stronger memories, cumulative tests help students to improve the connections they make between information taught at the beginning of the course and the information that comes later. These connections are among the

most important aspects of their learning because they create a complete pattern of understanding.

3. **Have students spend time in reflection.** Memory for nonarousing positive or negative stimuli may benefit from conscious encoding strategies, such as elaboration. This elaboration processing can be autobiographical or semantic (Kensinger, 2004). One powerful form of elaboration is reflection. I believe that reflection is the lost art of college learning. It was lost when the information age descended upon us and faculty members were asked to add more and more content with no corresponding change in the time frame in which we teach. As my former chair once said, "We are stuffing 10 pounds of sausage into a 5-pound bag and wondering why things are falling through the cracks." The power of reflection is that it causes an increase in the number of connections our students can make between the new information they are learning and their prior knowledge. Each new connection offers an additional memory path for the new information. When we ask our students to consider how they can use what they have just learned to solve other problems, improve their own lives, or help others, or how it can be applied in new and imaginative ways, we are helping them form new connections for the information and deepening their understanding, too. Reflective questions in class or reflective journals outside class serve to promote long-term recall. Leo Buscaglia, the so-called love professor at the University of Southern California back in the 1970s, asked a teacher who he was visiting what the students were doing: They appeared to be just sitting doing nothing. She replied, "This is their thinking time."

4. **Ask students to explain what they have learned in their own words.** John Ratey, in his book *A User's Guide to the Brain*, describes the human brain as a pattern-seeking device that is constantly looking for how new information fits with the patterns of prior knowledge (Ratey, 2001). What is the most familiar pattern our students have? It is their personal language. When we ask our students to tell us in their own words what something means or how it works, we are asking them to translate a new pattern into a familiar one. There are two major benefits of this process. First is the immediate recognition of the degree to which our students understand the new information: If they can't translate it into their own words, they don't understand it. Second is the creation of a new pattern that is more familiar and

therefore easier to recall, especially when students use their own examples or metaphors to explain the new information. Getting students to use familiar patterns is one key to improving long-term recall. We can formalize this process by asking our students to write summaries of lectures or text material in their own words.

5. **Use as much visual information as possible.** We have already discussed the power of images earlier in the book. Using images to illustrate the ideas and concepts we teach enhances our learners' ability to understand and remember. The last few pages of this chapter contain a list of strategies for helping students better remember their course information. Note that visualizing the information is one of these strategies. We can help this visualization by including images that reinforce and/or clarify what we teach.

Make the Learning Personal and Emotional to Improve Recall

Emotion is devoted to an organism's survival. (Damasio, 2001)

On the first day of my daughter's college chemistry class, the professor poured alcohol on the top of her desk and lit it on fire. She did so to gain the attention of the students and to demonstrate that some of the learning in the class was going to be surprising, fun, and informative. My daughter, now 27, still talks about that day and how much she enjoyed that chemistry class. The teacher's fiery demonstration was an example of two very important tools in the formation of memory. One was attention and the other was emotion; in this case, the emotion was surprise! We cannot hope to teach our students anything if we do not have their attention. Attention is absolutely necessary for learning. How we get their attention and hold it determines in great part how successful we are as teachers. We can never spend too much time planning ways to get and hold our students' attention. It is the first crucial step to helping them make memories of what they learn.

Various factors increase or decrease the amount of attention students will pay to us. These factors include distinctiveness, affective valence, prevalence, complexity, and functional value. In addition, the characteristics of the students themselves, such as sensory capacities, arousal level, perceptual set, and past reinforcement, also affect their attention (Bandura, 1997). Emotional arousal appears to increase the likelihood of memory consolidation during the retention (storage) stage of memory. A number of studies show that, over time, memories for neutral stimuli decrease but memories for arousing stimuli remain the same or improve (LaBar & Phelps, 1998). Other studies have discovered that memory enhancements for emotional information tend to be greater after longer delays than after relatively short ones. This delayed effect is consistent with the proposal that emotionally arousing memories are more likely to be converted into a relatively permanent trace, whereas memories for nonarousing events are more vulnerable to disruption (Heuer & Reisberg, 1990). Emotional valence alone can enhance memory; that is, non-arousing items with positive or negative valence can be better remembered than neutral items (Ochsner, 2000). The power of emotional memories may date back a long time. For our ancestors, the thrill of finding food or the fear of prowling predators could have started the pattern (Pert, 1997).

Helping Our Students Improve Their Memories

One of the most important aspects of moving from a teacher-centered to a learner-centered approach is helping our students to improve their learning and study abilities. Asking students to do more of the work includes an obligation to teach them how to improve their own learning processes so they can become independent, lifelong learners. The following 10 suggestions are taken from the literature of cognitive psychology and neuroscience, and we can share these suggestions with our students to help them improve their memory processes.

1. **Focus your attention on the materials you are studying.** Attention is king. No learning happens without attending to the input stimuli. The brain works best when it is focused on just one task. Trying to multitask hurts learning, increases errors, and adds time to the completion of a task (Foerde, Knowlton, & Poldrack, 2006).

2. **Don't cram for exams.** Cramming is a hollow victory for students. Yes, they can get a passing grade or even earn an A by cramming, but the research makes clear that little of the information ever makes its way into long-term memory (Bjork, 2001). The key is practice over time. Research has shown that students who study regularly remember the material far better that those who did all of their studying in one marathon session, especially when trying to recall it days or weeks later (Bjork, 2001).

3. **Structure and organize the information.** Researchers have found that information is organized in memory in related clusters. Students

need to group similar concepts and terms together, or make an outline of their notes and textbook readings to help group related concepts.

4. **Mnemonic devices can help.** A mnemonic is simply any technique that aids recall. The most familiar are HOMES (for remembering the Great Lakes: Huron, Ontario, Michigan, Erie, and Superior) and Every Good Boy Deserves Favor (for remembering the music scale of EGBDF). These devices can use any sensory process. The idea is to have the device connect with something that students already know well or is easy to learn. Many students make up songs to remember large amounts of scientific information (for example, visit YouTube and search for songs about the periodic table).

5. **Elaborate and rehearse information.** As I mentioned earlier in this chapter, elaborative rehearsal is an important strategy for improving recall. Effective elaborations include reflection activities, mapping of information, creating images for the information, annotating assigned readings, writing and rewriting notes, and summarizing or paraphrasing.

6. **Relate new information to prior knowledge.** Our students need to make a conscious effort to connect the patterns of their new information to what they already know, especially by using familiar patterns such as similarity and difference, cause and effect, and comparison and contrast. By connecting new information to prior knowledge, they increase the likelihood of understanding it and recalling it (Bjork, 2001).

7. **Visualize concepts.** Images are easy for our brain to understand and recall (Zull, 2002). We need to remind our students of this again and again.

8. **Teach new concepts to another person.** I devoted a chapter in another of my books to the powerful learning that can take place when students teach each other. The level of preparation they need to engage in teaching and the act of telling and showing others strengthens understanding and recall (Lepper & Woolverton, 2002).

9. **Pay extra attention to information in the middle of class.** Many researchers have found that the likelihood of recalling information presented at the beginning and end of class is easier than information presented in the middle of class. This is often referred to as the serial position effect. The improved recall of information at the beginning of class is often referred to as the primacy effect; the improved recall

of information at the end of class is referred to as the recency effect. Because of these findings, it is especially important to remind students of the need to stay focused throughout the entire class period. We can assist them by making certain we do something in our teaching to grab their attention during the middle of the class period.

10. **Vary your study routine.** Another great way that students may increase their recall is to change their study routine occasionally. If they are accustomed to studying in one specific location, they may want to try moving to a different spot to study. If they study in the evening, they should try to spend a few minutes each morning reviewing the information they studied the previous night. By adding an element of novelty to study sessions, students can increase the effectiveness of their efforts and improve their long-term recall (Bjork, 2001).

What Students Have Been Doing Likely Needs to Change

One of the most important messages we can share with our students is to follow the new science findings about how humans learn and remember. Most of our students have used the same memorizing and studying processes for so long that they either don't want to make the effort to change or can't see any reason to change. We need to help them understand that details such as getting enough sleep, taking naps, allowing some time between assigned classes, using all of one's senses to study, and many other findings that I have written about in this chapter are not just suggestions to be considered and then ignored. These are researched facts about how the human brain learns and remembers. We need to help our students to begin learning in harmony with their brains.

11

IS A REVOLUTION COMING?

Movement, Exercise, and Learning

The sedentary character of modern life is a disruption of our nature, and it poses one of the biggest threats to our continued survival.

(Ratey, 2008)

When I was 15, I went out for the varsity basketball team. My brother, who was the best player in the history of our high school, had graduated, so I thought there was room now for a new Doyle on the team. I also decided to try out because I knew I needed to get in better shape. Although I never approached my brother's success in basketball, I did discover something that has helped me to be a better learner my whole life. I discovered that when I ran a lot (and we ran *a lot*), I was always able to focus on school activities, particularly homework, better than when I was not in basketball season. I don't want you to think that somehow, at age 15, I knew exercise was important for learning; I didn't. I just recognized that it was easier to do my homework after basketball practice than it was other times of the year. Forty-five years later, I now have a scientific explanation about why my studying was easier: It was the neurochemicals serotonin, dopamine, and norepinephrine and the protein brain-derived neurotrophic factor (BDNF) that my brain released during my running that helped to improve my focus and learning (Ratey, 2008).

This chapter explores how exercise and movement play a vital role in learning, a role so significant that, regardless of how difficult it might be to find ways to integrate it into our learning protocols, it must be done at all levels of education.

What Science Says About Exercise and Learning

If we step back 500 million years ago, when the first nerve cells developed, we would discover that the original need for a nervous system was to coordinate movement so an organism could find food instead of waiting for the food to come to it. The first animals to experience movement had a tremendous advantage over sponges, for example, which had to wait brainlessly for dinner to arrive (Franklin Institute, 2004). Though a great deal of our evolutionary history remains shrouded in controversy, one thing paleoanthropologists agree on is that we moved (Medina, 2008). Anthropologist Richard Wrangham says that, a few hundred thousand years ago, men moved about 10 to 20 kilometers a day and women moved about half of that each day. Our brains developed while we were moving. In fact, it would be fair to say that our brains developed to solve problems of survival while humans were outdoors and in constant motion (Medina, 2008, p. 32).

Flash-forward to 1995 and Carl Cotman, director of the Institute for Brain Aging and Dementia at the University of California at Irvine, discovers that exercise sparks the master molecule of the learning process: brain-derived neurotrophic factor (BDNF), which is a protein produced inside nerve cells when they are active. BDNF serves as fertilizer for brain cells, keeping them functioning and growing; it also spurs the growth of new neurons (Ratey, 2008). With this discovery, Cotman showed a direct biological connection between movement and cognition (as cited in Ratey, 2008, p. 43). What Cotman first discovered in 1995 has blossomed into a revolution in terms of scientific study. In 1995, barely a handful of studies on BDNF existed. Today, more than 6,000 papers have been written on BDNF. John Ratey, author of *Spark: The Revolutionary New Science of Exercise and the Brain* (2008), referred to BDNF as "Miracle Grow for the brain." Ratey said, "Exercise strengthens the cellular machinery of learning by creating BDNF which gives synapses the tools they need to take in information, process it, associate, remember it and put it in context" (p. 45). UCLA neuroscientist Fernando Gómez-Pinilla's research shows that a brain low on BDNF shuts itself off to new information (Ying, Vaynman, & Gomez-Pinilla, 2004).

How Does Exercise Help Learning?

No matter your age, it seems, a strong, active body is crucial for building a strong, active mind. (Carmichael, 2007)

Exercise increases synaptic plasticity by directly affecting synaptic structure and potentiating synaptic strength, and by strengthening the underlying systems that support plasticity, including neurogenesis, metabolism, and vascular function (Cotman, Carl, Berchtold, & Christie, 2007). This very technical explanation means that exercise helps all of the key brain functions needed to make learning easier. Human and nonhuman animal studies have shown that aerobic exercise can improve many aspects of cognition and performance (Hillman, Erickson, & Kramer, 2008). In a 2011 *Newsweek* article, neuroscientist Yaakov Stern of Columbia University discussed the three events that occur in our brains and enhance our cognitive capacity. The first is an increase in number of neurons or synapses. The second is higher levels of neurogenesis (new cell growth), especially in the memory-forming hippocampus. The third is increased production of BDNF, which stimulates the production of neurons and synapses (as cited in Begley, 2011). All three occur when we exercise. Exercise itself doesn't make you smarter, but it puts the brain of the learners in the optimal position for them to learn (Ratey, 2008).

By exercise, I am referring to a wide variety of activities, with the most beneficial being aerobic exercise that also involves the learning of a new skill, such as learning to play tennis, learning one of the martial arts, or even practicing a new dance step. Any movement is better than no movement when it comes to enhancing learning. Many studies show the positive effects of simple walking on improved cognitive functioning, especially in older adults (Weuve et al., 2008).

Brain-Derived Neurotrophic Factor and Exercise

Brain-derived neurotrophic factor (BDNF) is a protein that gathers in reserve pools near synapses in our brains and is unleashed when we get our blood pumping. BDNF generates new neurons, protects existing neurons, and promotes synaptic plasticity, which is generally considered the basis for learning and memory (Mattson, Wenzhen, Rugian, & Gou, 2004; Modie, 2003). In this process, a number of hormones, including insulin-like growth factor, vascular endothelial growth factor, and fibroblast growth factor from our bodies, are called into action to help the BDNF crank up the molecular machinery of learning (Ratey, 2008, p. 52). All of this brain activity results in learning that is improved on three levels.

Level One

Exercise increases the production of three very important neurochemicals involved in learning: serotonin, dopamine, and norepinephrine. These neurochemicals aid our brains in their ability to be alert, pay attention, be motivated for learning, and be positive toward learning (improve mood), and they help to enhance our patience and self-control (Ratey, 2008). As educators, we know that these abilities are crucial to successful learning. Perhaps most significant is that the areas improved by exercise are the very areas where many of our students struggle most in their learning. If our students are alert, focused, motivated, and paying attention; had positive attitudes; and could manage their in-class behaviors appropriately, it might be fair to say that we have the perfect learning situation.

Level Two

Exercise prepares and encourages nerve cells to bind to one another, which is the cellular basis for logging in new information (Ratey, 2008, p. 53). Exercise stimulates the production of new synapses, whose capacity and efficiency underlie superior intelligence (Kramer et al., 2010). Put simply, exercise makes it easier for us to grow smarter. One piece of evidence that supports this finding comes from a 1999 study done in the Naperville, Illinois, public schools, where aerobic exercise was added to the junior high school curriculum. Results show significant increases in students' test score performance, even on tests like the Trends in International Mathematics and Science Study (TIMSS), on which most often U.S. schools rank well below their worldwide counterparts. The Naperville eighth-grade students finished first in the world in science, just ahead of Singapore, and sixth in math (trailing Singapore, South Korea, Taiwan, Hong Kong, and Japan) (Ratey, 2008, p. 14). Yes, these were middle-class youngsters from a good school system, but they did not match neighboring schools in per pupil funding or in average scores on college entrance exams (SAT or ACT). There was nothing to suggest that this kind of accomplishment was in their future. TIMSS is the same test in which only 7% of U.S. students even scored in the top tier. An additional positive, albeit unexpected, finding from the study showed a 66% decline in behavior problems and suspensions following the introduction of aerobic activities at the school. This was associated with the positive effect that the neurochemicals of serotonin, dopamine, and noradrenalin had on students' ability to control their behavior.

Level Three

Exercise also spurs the development of new nerve cells, in a process called neurogenesis, from stem cells in the hippocampus (Ratey, 2008, p. 53). Prior to 1998, there was no conclusive evidence that our brains even made new cells. Once proof was established (Eriksson et al., 1998), scientists have been working to uncover what these new brain cells actually do. One discovery is that new cells spawned during exercise are better equipped to spark long-term potentiation (LTP), which is a long-lasting enhancement in signal transmission between two neurons that results from stimulating them synchronously. LTP is widely considered to be one of the major cellular mechanisms that underlie learning and memory (Cooke & Bliss, 2006). Princeton neuroscientist Elizabeth Gould suggested that these new cells play a role in hanging onto our conscious thoughts, while the prefrontal cortex decides if they should be wired in as long-term memories (Gould, 2008). Columbia University Medical Center neurologist Scott Small and Salk Institute neurobiologist Fred Gage (Small & Gage, 2007) found that the new neurons created by exercise cropped up in only one place: the dentate gyrus of the hippocampus, an area that controls learning and memory. The hippocampus is especially responsive to the effects of BDNF, and exercise seems to restore it to a healthier, "younger" state (Small & Gage, 2007). At this time, research continues as to the exact role(s) neurogenesis plays in our learning. What we do know for certain is that exercise promotes neurogenesis.

How Much Exercise Is Needed?

How much exercise is needed to experience the learning benefits already described in this chapter? This question has not been fully answered. One thing that is clear, however, is that trying to learn something that is difficult or complex *while* engaged in aerobic activity is a bad idea. When engaged in aerobic activity, blood flows away from the prefrontal cortex and hampers executive functioning. Once exercise is completed, however, blood flow returns to the prefrontal cortex almost immediately, and this is an ideal time for learning to take place. This is an important finding to share with students. Despite my best efforts to help my students understand the learning benefits of exercise, I still find some who think that, if exercise is good for learning, then trying to study during exercise must be a good idea.

Ratey suggests that 30 minutes of exercise in which our heart rates reach the appropriate levels for our age, four to five times a week, is a good baseline. The appropriate heart rate level is different for all of us. To figure mine, I subtract my age, which is 59, from 220, which it gives me my maximum heart rate per minute of 161. I should reach 60 to 70% of that level while exercising. In addition, if I can include in my aerobic-level workout the learning of a new skill, such as a new dance or martial art, this new skill would be even more beneficial for my brain (as cited in Begley, 2011). A study completed in 2007 showed that even one aerobic session lasting 35 minutes improved mental processing speeds and cognitive flexibility in adults (Carles et al., 2007). Neuroscientist Art Kramer and his colleagues at the University of Illinois found that a year of aerobic exercise can give a 70-year-old the connectivity of a 30-year-old, improving memory, planning, navigating of ambiguity, and multitasking (Kramer et al., 1999). In a study done on young and middle-aged adults, the authors found that physical activity may be beneficial to cognition during early and middle periods of the human lifespan and may continue to protect against age-related loss of cognitive function during older adulthood (Hillman et al., 2008). Neuroscientist Khatri Blumenthal and his colleagues reported that exercise had its beneficial effect in specific areas of cognitive function that are rooted in the frontal and prefrontal regions of the brain. The implications are that exercise might be able to offset some of the mental declines we often associate with the aging process (Blumenthal et al., 2001).

Using Exercise in School

When new ideas about how learning can be improved come along, there is always some reticence to jump on board. Educators have been led down paths to nowhere before. A prime example is in the right brain/left brain learning protocols that turned out to be unsupported by research findings but still found their way into all kinds of schools (Taylor, 2009). In the case of exercise, the research is solid, and implementation has been underway for the last 5 years. Next I describe several studies that show how exercise in schools is improving learning.

City Park High School in Saskatoon, Canada, put treadmills and exercise bikes in a math classroom; before doing any math, the kids strapped on their heart-rate monitors and did 20 minutes of moderate-intensity cardio-vascular exercise. This is an alternative school for students with learning difficulties, and over half the students have attention deficit hyperactivity disorder (ADHD). They couldn't sit still, many had behavioral problems, and they had difficulty learning. Within 5 months nearly all of the students had jumped a full letter grade in reading, writing, and math. After doing the exercise, the students were suddenly able to sit still and focus on what they were learning, and they were able to understand what they were being taught. The exercise altered their brain chemistry enough to make learning possible, *and* it greatly improved their behavior (Gurd, 2009).

In 2007, neuroscientist Charles Hillman described how he put 259 Illinois third-graders and fifth-graders through standard physical education routines such as push-ups and a timed run, and he measured their body mass. Then he checked their physical results against their math and reading scores on the Illinois Standards Achievement Test. The more physical tests they passed, the better they scored on the achievement test. The effects appeared regardless of gender and socioeconomic differences, so it seems that, regardless of his or her gender or family income, the fitness of a child's body and mind are closely linked (Hillman & Castelli, 2007a).

The bigger the dose of exercise, the more it can pay off in academic achievement. In a 2007 study, researchers found that children ages 7 to 11 who exercised for 40 minutes daily after school had greater academic improvement than children of the same age who worked out for just 20 minutes (Castelli, Hillman, Buck, & Erwin, 2007).

Getting Exercise and Movement in Higher Education

The challenge that confronts those of us in higher education is how we use these findings about exercise, movement, and learning to optimize our students' learning. We cannot turn our backs on this research simply because our schools' physical facilities are not conducive to letting students move around while learning. We need to approach this problem with the same creative, imaginative problem-solving processes that we constantly say we want our students to learn to use in their own lives. We talk the problem-solving talk to our students all the time; now we need to walk the walk.

In chapter 1, I briefly discuss a study at Grand Valley State University in Michigan where students sat on exercise balls instead of chairs while taking their science courses. Although qualitative in nature, findings were overwhelmingly positive because students reported that they felt they were better focused and learned more. This is an example of a starting place for introducing more movement into higher education. Starting in the fall of 2011, I will be doing a small research project using balance balls in my first-year reading courses. I am interested in finding out if the balance balls will help my students to stay more focused and on-task longer when reading, which is always a problem for them. In a recent visit to San Jacinta Community College in Houston, I was pleasantly surprised to see minibicycles under each of the computer tables in their students' computer lab. The coordinator said that the students enjoy the movement while working on their assignments and reported that they stay more engaged for longer periods of time.

One question I ask faculty members as I visit campuses is, How can we get more movement into our students' learning? The following are a few of their suggestions:

1. **Moving discussions.** Rather than have students sit and talk, have them walk and talk. It works by assigning students discussion questions and asking them to take a walk for 15 to 20 minutes and talk about the issues assigned. When they return, they sit down, record their findings, and then share them with the other groups.

2. **Walking critiques.** Have students complete a set of problems or answered questions on whiteboards or newsprint and then post the findings around the classroom. Students then walk around the room critiquing the findings of their peers, adding or changing answers as they walk along. When the critiques are completed, a discussion is held to determine the best answers based on the critiquing process.

3. **Guided tour.** Using the museum or national parks model of a walking tour, course lessons are taught while walking and observing items relevant to the course information. This technique works well in art, ecology, geography, architecture, and many other subjects.

4. **Allowing students to stand and stretch when needed during class.** I allow my students to do this any time they feel they are losing their attention. I have not found it to be disruptive, and I know that no reading is accomplished without full attention.

5. **Taking more breaks during lectures.** A significant number of studies prove a shortening of attention spans, especially since the flooding of the marketplace with personal media tools and toys (Swing, Gentile, Anderson, & Walsh, 2010). One way to help our students to focus is to let them move and breathe for periods of time as short as 30 seconds. Our brains need a lot of oxygen to function well, so letting students stretch, move, and breathe is good for learning. In addition, when a new concept has been introduced, students need an opportunity to practice thinking in terms of that concept. Letting them rise, stretch, and think about what they have just learned by generating their own examples of the concept, summarizing it, thinking of an exam question for it, or explaining it to someone else is part of the mind's natural processes of learning (Middendorf & Kalish, 1996).

Selling Our Students on the Value of Exercise

The more time I spent reading the research on exercise and learning, the more it became clear to me that I had to take meaningful actions. One such action was to begin my own aerobic exercise program that included learning new skills as part of the workout. The second was to work very hard to sell my students on the importance of putting exercise into their daily lives. To be honest, I have done much better on the latter of these two actions. I now do a 1-hour presentation in all of my classes about the relationship among exercise, movement, and learning. I detail the science behind it, showing how exercise leads to enhanced learning. I use the example of the junior high students from Naperville, Illinois, who finished first in the world in science on the TIMSS test after aerobics were introduced to the daily school activities. I have posted the slides I use from this presentation on my website, http://learnercenteredteaching.wordpress.com, for anyone who would like to have a similar discussion with their students. I have also created a video, available on YouTube, called "Exercise and College Learning" that can be shown to students. This research has the potential to improve learning in higher education significantly, and we have an obligation not only to share it with our students, but to sell it to them as a product they cannot do without.

12

GETTING OTHERS TO EMBRACE LEARNER-CENTERED TEACHING

[T]he moment has surely come for America's
colleges to take a more candid look at their
weaknesses and think more boldly about setting
higher educational standards for themselves.

(Bok, 2006)

I am a rock, I am an island, and a rock feels no
pain and an island never cries.

(Simon, 1966)

As I have heard from instructors on almost every campus I have visited
in the past several years, adopting a learner-centered practice can
cause faculty members to encounter resistance and criticism and to
receive lower teacher evaluation marks. To counter these reactions, it is necessary to explain the value of the learning-centered teaching (LCT)
approach. This brief chapter is designed to help you do just that.

I see three distinct groups who may have concerns about the use of LCT
practice. In all three cases, their concerns are usually a result of the lack of
information about LCT, although some criticize LCT even when they do
understand it. These people are usually the ones who do not want to face
change.

The first of the three resistant groups are administrators, who may evaluate your teaching without understanding a learner-centered approach and
therefore give you low marks. It is one of the oddities in higher education
that often those people designated to evaluate teachers don't teach and are

often far removed from the research on teaching and learning. Several faculty members have told me that their administrator said to them, "I will come back on a day when you are teaching." Of course, this is not true of all administrators, but after visiting 60 campuses and hearing this same concern again and again, I think it is a real issue.

Second are your colleagues, who may criticize you or hold tenure or promotion over your head because they are threatened by your approach. They may hold the mindset that they may have to change if LCT is a better approach, and they don't want to change. Some truly don't understand how an LCT approach can enhance learning. Maybe they were instructed that good teaching is synonymous with effective lecturing. It may also come from selective recall, in which they talk about the students they taught who have gone on to do great things, thereby believing that their traditional approach is validated. The fact that college graduation rates have declined over the past 30 years may suggest otherwise (Brainard & Fuller, 2010).

Third are your students. They will complain to you and your department chair about the amount of work they are being asked to do and suggest that you are not "teaching them," which is what "they are paying you to do." In their defense, our students come from high schools that still use traditional, teacher-centered education, so this is what they know and what they expect to see in college (U.S. Department of Education, 2001). These three groups all present different agendas regarding the implementation of a new teaching approach, but they also share some of the same concerns. Although I address administrators and colleagues as one group and students as a separate group, you will find that their concerns overlap in places and therefore so do my suggestions on how to help them understand an LCT approach. For example, both groups share a resistance based on fear of change. LCT-focused educators can address this fear effectively.

Understanding Change and Higher Education

Change is never simple or without its resisters. Almost 50 years ago, Thomas Kuhn's (1962) seminal work, *The Structure of Scientific Revolutions*, described how society responds when there is a significant shift in the prevailing paradigm. Kuhn argued that such a shift is typically met with vehement denial and opposition. It is not surprising that some, perhaps many, in higher education would not warm to the idea of another pedagogical change. It seems slow change is in our campus DNA. Ask any information technology person who has the newest, fastest, and most sophisticated software to help students learn or the university become more efficient about getting faculty members on board or campus offices to change their reporting procedures. They will tell you it is like getting your children to clean their room: difficult and frustrating.

Formal changes in higher education are often the product of long discussions and negotiations, also often involving institutionalized governance entities like departments or a faculty senate. Being wary of changing to a new instructional model does come with some legitimacy. Many "new" models of instruction have been proposed over the past 60 years, and they have come and gone, sometimes within only a year or two. For example, in the area of English language pedagogy, all of the following have been used since the 1940s: audiolingual method, counseling, direct method, grammar translation, silent way, and situational language teaching. One can see how caution signs might be thrown up when another new teaching idea comes around.

Why Have New Approaches Not Delivered?

Why did so many teaching approaches fail to produce the improved learning they promised? I think Robert Sylwester captured it perfectly when he said that the information upon which we made our teaching decisions was much closer to folklore than science (Sylwester, 1995, p. 5). I am not trying to disparage cognitive scientists or educational researchers who provided us their very best ideas about how we should instruct our students. I am simply pointing out that, without being able to look inside the human brain, the organ of learning, it was not possible to know how humans really learned. I have to go no further than my own experience as a reading teacher. I believed, as many did, that a whole language approach was the best way to proceed, only to discover 25 years later through brain-imaging studies that phonics is absolutely essential to the development of good readers. What makes a learner-centered practice different than all of the other teaching approaches is that it's based on science, not folklore. Each of us who believe in optimizing our students' learning must begin both the defense of our pedagogy and our advocacy of its acceptance by all.

Early Adopters

Sometimes it is not easy to be the first one on your block with a new approach to teaching. Every teaching method ever tried has helped someone to learn, even if it left many other learners unfulfilled or, even worse, completely lost. Those using a particular method can point to the success they had with some students. However, John Bransford (2000) points out in his book *How People Learn* that "many people who had difficulty in school might have prospered if the new ideas about effective instructional practices had been available. Furthermore, given new instructional practices, even those who did well in traditional educational environments might have developed skills, knowledge, and attitudes that would have significantly enhanced their achievements" (pp. 5–6). If you embrace a learner-centered approach but feel you are alone in embracing this approach within your college, I offer the following suggestions on how to defend yourself *and* promote LCT among your administrators, colleagues, and students.

Administrators and Colleagues

Step One: Obligation to Research

What one very important characteristic do our administrators have in common with our faculty colleagues that can help us to defend and promote LCT? The answer is that, in graduate school, they learned the importance of doing careful and accurate research and in using research findings to guide their practice. To be true to this training, our colleagues and administrators have an obligation to follow where the research leads them. The neuroscience, biology, and cognitive science research that supports having students engage in active, authentic, and meaningful work as the best means to enhance their learning is overwhelming. These research findings now appear in journals that integrate neuroscience research with the content study in almost every subject area taught in college (see the list of journals in Figure 12.1). Harvard University now offers a master's degree in Brain, Mind and Education. The most ardent supporters of the lecture method would need to be in total denial and never pick up a journal to believe that LCT is just another new teaching fad. Those who would suggest that we are not on the right path must be reminded of what Jean Lave and Etienne Wenger argued that all would-be scientists, mathematicians, engineers, and historians need to be "enculturated" into the discipline—and the earlier, the better (Lave & Wenger, 1991). Instead of educators and students being told about science or math, they actually *do* science and math—really live it.

The argument to be made here is the most important message in this book: The one who does the work does the learning. If students are to

FIGURE 12.1
New Journals Integrating Neuroscience and Content Study

- *Journal of Cognitive Neuroscience*
- *Nature Neuroscience*
- *Journal of Computational Neuroscience*
- *Journal of Medicine, Social Cognition and Affective Neuroscience*
- *Behavioral Neuroscience*
- *Journal of Neuroscience Nursing*
- *Visual Neuroscience*
- *Journal of Neuroscience and Behavioral Health*
- *Journal of Neuroscience Psychology and Economics*
- *Journal of Mathematics Neuroscience*
- *Chemical Neuroscience*
- *Biological Psychiatry*
- *Nutritional Neuroscience*
- *Journal of Social Neuroscience*
- *Arts Neuroscience*

maximize their learning abilities, which means, by definition, firing and wiring their neurons over a long enough period of time to have these neuron-networks become long-term memories, they must be engaged in learning activities that enhance their understanding and cause them to practice the material long enough to learn it. They cannot be passive observers of learning. In addition to the scientific evidence I outlined in chapter 1, you can find additional evidence on my website, www.learnercenteredteaching.word press.com. You can use this evidence to support a learner-centered teaching approach.

Step Two: Teaching Portfolio

Let's say it is my job to evaluate you as a learner-centered teacher. I cannot do that by observing you because all that is happening in your classroom is students working diligently in pairs or teams. They are solving authentic problems and preparing their findings for discussion and/or presentation to classmates or an outside professional. If this is what I see when I visit your classroom, then I need something else to review. That something else is a teaching portfolio. Every teacher who seeks to be outstanding in her or his profession should have a teaching portfolio regardless of pedagogical preferences. The portfolio should include the following: a written description of your teaching philosophy, research support for the instructional methods you use in your teaching, a list of learning outcomes for each course, the course syllabi, lesson plans for each course activity that include a list of the resources students use, a description of your assessment methods, and examples of assessment tools. The portfolio should also include findings from ongoing informal feedback from students about the effectiveness of the learning activities, formal teacher evaluations (if available), peer support letters for your teaching methods, and any formal assessment measures used by your department or college (if they exist).

The portfolio represents your teaching. It explains why and how you are facilitating students' learning and how you prove that you are being successful. It is hard evidence of your planning abilities, level of preparedness, and grounding in appropriate research for the methods chosen. It shows that you value the need for quality assessment to validate that learning took place. Providing an administrator or colleague with this portfolio allows him or her to understand more fully what it means to be a learned-centered teacher. It also removes any doubt that the activities you facilitate in your classroom are anything less than the highest quality of teaching.

Is this a lot of work? Yes, at least initially. However, it is the kind of work any effective teacher does anyway. I know of no better way to defend LCT and to help others understand how we are optimizing our students' learning than through a well-constructed portfolio.

Step Three: Discussion

My friend and long-time dean of our College of Arts and Sciences, Matt Klein, implemented a program for first-year tenure-track faculty evaluation that included a face-to-face discussion about teaching. New faculty members meet with Matt and members of their tenure committee to discuss what the tenure committee would like to see as evidence of their teaching abilities before formal evaluation begins. In addition, new faculty members are offered an opportunity to share with the dean and tenure committee members their philosophy of teaching and reasons for the methods they use, as well as prepare the members for what they might see when they visit their classroom. In this way, Dean Klein has opened the door for research-based methods of instruction to be validated in the college.

We are a teaching institution, and I realize that many institutions still do not value teaching's role in granting tenure the way we do; however, I describe this process because this is how anyone, administrator or faculty member, concerned about doing effective teacher evaluations should proceed. Anyone concerned about how their LCT approach may be perceived by administrators or colleagues may want to ask for a face-to-face discussion before any formal evaluation process begins. It is not only a great way to ensure that those doing the evaluation understand how students' learning will be taking place in your courses, but it is also a chance to educate others to the value of an LCT approach.

Step Four: Training

The Faculty Center for Teaching and Learning here at Ferris State University was asked by the provost to provide all administrators with training to better understand learner-centered teaching. The center provided not only an overview of what LCT is and the research that supports its use but also gave specific suggestions about how to evaluate teachers who are using LCT. These recommendations included the following:

1. A face-to-face discussion about teaching philosophy and methodology.
2. The request for a teaching portfolio along the lines I just described.
3. Peer evaluations both from classroom observations and from face-to-face discussions about teaching approach.
4. Both informal (those given at the 5th and 10th week by the instructor to make certain students feel they are learning) and formal (those given by the university) student evaluations.

I provide this example from Ferris State University as a model for your institution to engage in the same kind of training. With assessment becoming such an important part of our higher education activities, it only seems reasonable that those in charge of assessing our teaching effectiveness at least understand learner-centered teaching and the overwhelming research supporting it.

Students

Step One: Explain Why

In my earlier book on learner-centered teaching, I made the case that the most important thing teachers must do to help students understand the LCT approach was to give students clear rationales for each and every learning activity and assignment. I divided the rationales into three areas:

1. An obligation to follow the research on teaching and student learning.

2. Preparation for the student's career path.
3. Preparation for the student's role as a lifelong learner.

In addition, I suggested that students be reminded daily that the reason they are being given more responsibility for their own learning (as demonstrated by the increased amount of choice and control they have in an LCT classroom) is because they will be responsible for their learning the rest of their lives.

Students, especially students who did well in traditional, teacher-centered high schools, will naturally be uncomfortable with an LCT approach. In their minds, they were rewarded for doing well in the traditional system, so why change it? This thought process, coupled with the fact that LCT requires more work and more responsibility than students were asked to do in a traditional classroom, is the reason why it is crucial to give students a clear, well-supported rationale for each and every activity and assignment throughout the semester. Although it is important to formally introduce the students to the research that supports LCT the first day of class, it is not enough; daily reminders are needed.

Step Two: Share the Research

Faculty members across the country have shared with me that, in their experience, presenting the actual research findings that describe how learning occurs in the human brain is a great place to start when building a convincing case for using an LCT approach. My own experiences reflect that, too. I have found students to be genuinely fascinated to see how the brain wires and fires its neurons and how quickly recall can be lost if extended practice over time does not occur. On my website, www.learnercenteredteaching. com, I have made available a PowerPoint presentation entitled "Learning in Harmony with Your Brain," which you are free to use with your students. This PowerPoint is what I use with my students and dozens of other student groups on our campus to help them understand how their brains learn and why LCT is the right approach to teaching them. Please use it with your students and refer to it throughout the semester in supporting the activities and assignments you use. I am always surprised and pleased when my students tell me that they have shared this research with their friends and family.

Step Three: We Are Getting You Ready for Your Career

Students are very good at asking, How is this course, assignment, or content going to help me in my job or career? or How is it relevant to my life? In fact, I would argue that these are two of their favorite questions. The second rationale to help support an LCT approach is that many of the learning activities and assignments used in such an approach are designed to help students develop their job and career skills. For example, if we left our campuses for a few weeks and observed our graduates at their jobs, we would see that the main skill set they use in the 'majority of their workday is that of talking with and listening to people. LCT activities that require students to discuss, work in teams and groups, give speeches and/or presentations, answer questions in class, explain their ideas to others, or to participate in any other learning activity that involves active communication are not only relevant to student job preparation but vital to their success in the workplace. We just need to keep reminding students of this.

What skills do companies, businesses, hospitals, and other workplaces want in graduates? Figure 12.2 lists the 12 essentials for success put together by the Career Services Network at Michigan State University. The list is highly reflective of most institutions' views on what our students need to be prepared for their careers. Using these 12 areas as rationales for learning activities and assignments is a great way to help students see that your LCT approach has their best interests at heart.

Step Four: Students Must See Themselves as Lifelong Learners

Lifelong learning is often viewed by students as something in the distant future, something they know will probably be necessary but that they do not need to be concerned with now. What makes LCT such an important instructional approach is that it seeks to prepare students to be lifelong learners, but it does so by using their current reality, the course they are in right now, as the vehicle. When you are 18 years old, it is often hard to imagine what life will be like when you are 25, let alone when you are 45 or 65. Learner-centered teaching seeks to prepare students to be lifelong learners by teaching them how to learn on their own, how to learn with and from others, how to find and use resources, how to determine what is important to know and what is not, and how to share ideas with others face to face and in a virtual environment. We need to remind students each day that the activities and assignments we use are not just for the immediate need of job preparation but also to prepare them for a future we have no way of knowing, except to know that they will desperately need a set of learning skills to cope with it. We need to remind them that the role of a college education has changed. A bachelor of arts or bachelor of science degree gives students only their "learner's permit." It is just the beginning of their learning journey—a journey that we know will require the learning skills we use in our

FIGURE 12.2

Michigan State University, Career Services Network: Twelve Competencies Essential for Success That Employers Seek in College Graduates

1. **Working in a diverse environment:** Learning from people who are different from you—and recognizing your commonalities.
2. **Managing time and priorities:** Managing how you spend your time, and on what, is essential in today's world.
3. **Acquiring knowledge:** Learning how to learn is just as important as the knowledge itself. You have to be a lifelong learner.
4. **Thinking critically:** Developing solid critical thinking skills means you'll be confident to handle autonomy, make sound decisions, and find the connection between opportunities.
5. **Communicating effectively:** Developing listening, interpreting, and speaking skills is just as important as reading and writing.
6. **Solving problems:** Understanding the process and mind-set of successful problem solving is essential for handling the bigger challenges that come your way.
7. **Contributing to a team:** In the workplace each person's contribution is essential to success. Having the ability to work collaboratively with others is vital. Working collaboratively includes identifying individual strengths (yours and others) and harnessing them for the group, building consensus, knowing when to lead and when to follow, and appreciating group dynamics.
8. **Navigating across boundaries:** Life is filled with boundaries—good and bad. Discover how to avoid the boundaries that become barriers so that you don't hamper your ability to collaborate with other people.
9. **Performing with integrity:** It takes only one bad instance to destroy years of good faith and good relationships. It's important to develop a code of ethics and principles to guide your life.
10. **Developing professional competencies:** Build on what you already know and keep learning new skills—your job will challenge you to grow and develop in ways you haven't imagined yet.
11. **Balancing work and life:** You've got a lot to accomplish in limited time. You must be able to get it all done and still stay sane.
12. **Embracing change:** Just about every aspect of life is in a constant state of change. Sometimes it may seem that no sooner do you get caught up than you have to start all over again. No matter how you feel about change, you have to learn to deal with it.

LCT classrooms. The U.S. Department of Labor reported in 2008 that a young person at age 18 could expect to have 10 to 14 different jobs by age 38 (U.S. Department of Labor, 2008). Reminding students that LCT prepares them for both the immediate world of work and the even longer-term future is an excellent way to get students to understand the validity of LCT.

A Final Point

The simple message of this chapter can be summed up in one word: *why*! Administrators, colleagues, and students need to know *why* we use LCT methods and how these methods translate into improved learning. If we can explain both points to these three groups of people, we will be well prepared to defend LCT and to be practicing advocates for its use.

Guidelines for Classroom Discussion

1. Everyone in class has both a right and an obligation to participate in discussions and, if called upon, is expected to respond.
2. Always listen carefully, with an open mind, to the contributions of others.
3. Ask for clarification when you don't understand a point someone has made.
4. If you challenge others' ideas, do so with factual evidence and appropriate logic.
5. If others challenge your ideas, be willing to change your mind if they demonstrate errors in your logic or use of the facts.
6. Don't introduce irrelevant issues into the discussion.
7. If others have made a point with which you agree, don't bother repeating it (unless you have something important to add).
8. Be efficient in your discourse; make your points and then yield to others.
9. Above all, avoid ridicule and try to respect the beliefs of others, even if they differ from yours. (The Guided Discussion, [1992, February], UNC Center for Teaching and Learning.)

Ground Rules for In-Class Small Group Discussion
Designed to Increase Group Accountability

1. Establish a timeline for the discussion (e.g., "You will have 20 minutes").
2. Assign a group leader. This position gets rotated with each new discussion.
3. Each member of the group must take notes. Group answers will be presented to the whole class.
4. Name(s) of the person(s) contributing to the answer are attached to each answer.
5. Teacher chooses person to report at random from each group.

6. Groups may be tested on the material.
7. Peer evaluation will be used.
8. Groups will be expected to ask questions and/or challenge the finds of other groups.
9. Assign a timekeeper. This job is designed to ensure the group completes its work.
10. Establish time limits on reporting.
11. All have an obligation to share what they know with group.
12. No use of slang, inappropriate language, name-calling, or accusations.
13. It is required to evaluate the findings of the other groups. (Developed by Professor Doyle's first year students for use in READ 106, 2010)

Basic Model of Group Discussion Guidelines

1. The first rule is to listen. This means, at a minimum, that only one person talks at a time.
2. The next rule is to include everyone.
3. The last rule is to speak to, not about, people. This means that no one who is not present can be mentioned by name, and no one who is present can be talked about in the third person—whether or not his or her name is used. Avoid all put-downs.

All three of these rules have moral importance and can be summarized by the one maxim: Be respectful.

Basic Group Roles

Facilitator (Task Oriented): Makes sure everyone participates. Doesn't let one person dominate the conversation or quiet students from sharing their ideas or opinions. Keeps everyone on task and focused on the agenda.

Time Keeper: Keeps track of the time allotted for the activity/discussion. Informs the group of time limitations.

Recorder: Writes the group responses on a sheet of paper or newspaper.

Reporter: Shares with the larger group the results, comments, or summaries of the discussion of the work group. (www.ccsf.edu/Resources/VOICE/ ... /group work/ ... /groupdiscussion.pdf)

Group Guidelines for Long Term Group Work

All members will attend all group meetings.

- Members will be prepared to share their assigned work with the group.
- Members will listen to each other and when necessary disagree or criticize in a professional and reasonable manner.
- Members will take seriously their obligation to contribute fully to the success of the group.
- Members will share equally in the tasks of preparing and completing the group's project.
- A specific set of consequences or penalties for failing to carry out the duties of the group will be outlined before group activity begins.
- A member of the group will be assigned to take notes of the group interaction.
- Each activity will begin with a purpose statement.
- Groups will be responsible for defining the vocabulary terms of the activity.
- Each group should be prepared to constructively criticize the other groups' findings.
- Each group member will recognize that the whole of the group is greater than the contributions of any one member. (Developed for READ 106 course, 2008, by students and Professor Doyle)

Anderson, L. W., & Krathwohl, D. R. (Eds.). (2001). *A taxonomy for learning, teaching and assessing: A revision of Bloom's taxonomy of educational objectives* (Complete ed.). New York: Longman.

Andrews, J. D. (1980). The verbal structure of teacher questions: Its impact on class discussion. *POD Quarterly, 2,* 130–163.

Arnsten, A. F. T., Paspalas, C. D., Gamo, N. J., Yang, Y., & Wang, M. (2010). Dynamic network connectivity: A new form of neuroplasticity. *Trends in Cognitive Sciences, 4,* 365–375.

Aronson, J. (2007). In "The secret to raising smart kids" by Carol Dweck. *Scientific American.* 29 Jul. Retrieved November 5, 2010, from http://homeworkhelpblog .com/the-secret-to-raising-smartkids/

Arum, R., & Roksa, J. (2011). *Academically adrift: Limited learning on college campuses.* Chicago: University of Chicago Press.

Atkins, D. (2007). Response to the article "Fixed mindset vs. growth mindset: Which one are you?" by Michael Graham Richard. Retrieved May 5, 2010, from http://michaelgr.com/2007/04/15/fixed-mindset-vs-growth-mindset-which-one-are-you/

Banaszynski, J. (2000). Teaching the American revolution: Scaffolding to success. *Education World: The Educator's Best Friend.* Retrieved November 1, 2010, from http://www.educationworld.com/a_curr/curr218.shtml

Bandura, A. (1997). *Self-efficacy: The exercise of control.* New York: W.H. Freeman.

Baram, T. Z., Chen, Y., Dubé, C. M., & Rice, C. J. (2008). Rapid loss of dendritic spines after stress involves derangement of spine dynamics by corticotropin-releasing hormone. *Journal of Neuroscience, 28,* 2903–2911.

Barrett, N. F. (1991). Cognitive styles and strategies. Unpublished. Retrieved January 22, 2011, from http://barrett-evaluations.com/_pdfs/cogstrategies.pdf

Barton, J., Heilker, P., & Rutkowsk, D. (2008). Fostering effective classroom discussions. Retrieved February 12, 2011, from http://www.utoledo.edu/centers/ctl/teaching_resources/Fostering _Effective_Classroom_Discussions.html

Begley, S., (2011). *Can You Build a Better Brain.* Retrieved June 10, 2011, from http://www.newsweek.com/2011/01/03/can-you-build-a-better-brain.html

Berman, M. G., Jonides, J., & Kaplan, S. (2008). The cognitive benefits of interacting with nature. *Psychological Science, 19,* 1207–1212.

Berman, M. G., & Kaplan, S. (2010). Directed attention as a common resource for executive functioning and self-regulation. *Perspectives on Psychological Science, 5*(1), 43–57.

Bibb, J. A., Mayford, M. R., Tsien, J. Z., & Alberini, C. M. (2010). Cognition enhancement strategies. *The Journal of Neuroscience, 10 November, 30*(45), 14987–14992.

Birbii, M., (2006). Mapping Knowledge: Concept Maps in Early Childhood Education." *Early Childhood Research & Practice, 8*(2). Retrieved on February 14, 2011, from http://ecrp.uiuc.edu/v8n2/birbili.html

Bjork, D. R. (1994). Memory and metamemory: Considerations in the training of human beings. In J. Metcalfe & A. Shimamura (Eds.), *Metacognition: Knowing about knowing,* 185–205. Cambridge, MA: MIT Press.

Bjork, D. (2001). How to succeed in college: Learn how to learn. *APS Observer, 14*(3), 9.

Bligh, D. A. (2000). *What's the use of lectures?* San Francisco, CA: Jossey-Bass.

Bloom, B. S., & Krathwohl, D. R. (1956). *Taxonomy of educational objectives: The classification of educational goals, by a committee of college and university examiners. Handbook 1: Cognitive domain.* New York: Longmans.

Blumenthal, K., Babyak, J. R., Craighead, A., Herman, W. E., Baldewicz, S., Madden, T., Doraiswamy, D. J., Waugh, T. M., & Krishnan, K. R. (2001). Effects of exercise training on cognitive functioning among depressed older men and women. *Journal of Aging and Physical Activity, 9,* 43–57.

Bohn, R., & Short, J. E. (2009). How much information? 2009 report on American consumers. Retrieved October 15, 2010, from http://hmi.ucsd.edu/pdf/HMI_2009_ConsumerReport_Dec9_2009.pdf

Bok, D. (2006). *Our underachieving colleges: A candid look at how much students learn and why they should be learning more.* Princeton, NJ: Princeton University Press.

Bottge, B. A., Rueda, E., Serlin, R., Hung, Y. H., & Kwon, J. (2007). Shrinking achievement differences with anchored math problems: Challenges and possibilities. *Journal of Special Education, 41,* 31–49.

Brainard, J., & Fuller, A. (2010). Graduation rates fall at one-third of 4-year colleges. *Chronicle of Higher Education.* Retrieved December 12, 2010, from http://chronicle.com/article/Graduation-Rates-Fall-at/125614/

Brain seeks patterns where none exist. (Pod cast). (2008). *Scientific American.* Retrieved November 13, 2010, from http://www.scientificamerican.com/podcast/episode.cfm?id = brain-seeks-patterns-where-none-exi-08-10-03

Bransford, J., National Research Council, Committee on Developments in the Science of Learning, National Research Council, & Committee on Learning Research and Educational Practice. (2000). *How people learn: Brain, mind, experience, and school* (Expanded ed.). Washington, DC: National Academy Press.

Brookfield, S., & Preskill, S. (1999). *Discussion as a way of teaching: Tools and techniques for democratic classrooms.* San Francisco, CA: Jossey-Bass.

Brookfield, S. D., & Preskill, S. (2005). *Discussion as a way of teaching: Tools and techniques for democratic classrooms* (2nd ed.). San Francisco, CA: Jossey-Bass.

Brown, G., & Atkins, M. (1988). *Effective teaching in higher education.* London: Methuen.

Brown, J. (1958). Some tests of the decay theory of immediate memory. *Quarterly Journal of Experimental Psychology, 10,* 12–21.

Brown, J. S. (1999). *Learning, working & playing in the digital age:* A speech given at the 1999 Conference on Higher Education of the American Association for Higher Education. Retrieved October 18, 2010, from http://www.ntlf.com/html/sf/jsbrown.pdf

Brown, J. S., Collins, A., & Duguid, P. (1989). Situated cognition and the culture of learning. *Educational Researcher, 18*(1), 32–42.

Bruffee, K. (1984). Collaborative learning and the conversation of mankind. *College English. 46*(7), 635–652.

Bruffee, K. (1993). *Collaborative learning: Higher education, interdependence and the authority of knowledge.* Baltimore, MD: Johns Hopkins University Press.

Caine, G., & Caine, R. (2006). Meaningful learning and the executive functions of the human brain. In S. Johnson & K. Taylor (Eds.), *The neuroscience of adult learning* (pp. 53–62). San Francisco, CA: Jossey-Bass.

Caine, G., McClintic, C., & Klimek, K. (2009). *12 Brain/mind learning principles in action.* Thousand Oaks, CA: Corwin Press.

Caine, R., & Caine, G. (1991). *Making connections: Teaching and the human brain.* Alexandria, VA: Association for Supervision and Curriculum Development.

Carles, S., Jr., Curnier, D., Pathak, A., Roncalli, J., Bousquet, M., Garcia, J., & Senard, J. (2007). Cardiac rehabilitation: Brief report effects of short-term exercise and exercise training on cognitive function among patients with cardiac disease. *Journal of Cardiopulmonary Rehabilitation & Prevention, 27*(6), 395–399. doi:10.1097/01.HCR.0000300268.00140.e6

Carmichael, M. (2007). Stronger, faster, smarter. *Newsweek,* March 26, 38–46.

Carnegie Mellon Learning Principles. (2011). Retrieved January 24, 2011, from http://www.cmu.edu/teaching/principles/learning.html

Cashman, T. G. (2007). Issues-centered projects for classrooms in the United States and Mexico borderlands. *Journal of Authentic Learning, 4*(1), 9–24.

Cassady, J. C., & Johnson, R. (2002). Cognitive test anxiety and academic performance. *Contemporary Educational Psychology, 27*(2), 270–295.

Castelli, D., Hillman, C., Buck, S., & Erwin, H. (2007). Physical fitness and academic achievement in 3rd and 5th grade students. *Journal of Spots and Exercise Psychology, 29,* 239–252.

Chamberlin, S. A., & Moon, S. (2005). Model-eliciting activities: An introduction to gifted education. *Journal of Secondary Gifted Education, 17,* 37–47.

Chan, J. C., McDermott, K. B., & Roediger, H. L. (2007). Retrieval-induced facilitation. *Journal of Experimental Psychology: General, 135*(4), 553–571.

Charbonnier, E., Huguet, P., Brauer, M., & Monte, J. (1998). Social loafing and self-beliefs: People's collective effort depends on the extent to which they distinguished themselves as better than others. *Social Behavior and Personality, 26*(4), 329–340. doi:10.2224/sbp.1998.26.4.329.

Cherry, K. (2010). Explanations for forgetting. Retrieved June 8, 2011, from http://psychology.about.com/od/cognitivepsychology/tp/explanations-for-forgetting.htm

Chickering, A. W., & Gamson, Z. F. (1991). Applying the seven principles for good practice in undergraduate education. *New Directions for Teaching and Learning, 47*, 51–61.

Collier, K. G. (1980). Peer-group learning in higher education: The development of higher-order skills. *Studies in Higher Education, 5*(1), 55–62.

Cooke, S. F., & Bliss, T. V. (2006). Plasticity in the human central nervous system. *Brain, 129*(7), 1659–1673. doi:10.1093/brain/awl082.PMID_16672292

Cooper, J., & Associates. (1990). *Cooperative learning and college instruction.* Long Beach: Institute for Teaching and Learning, California State University.

Cooperative Institutional Research Program. (1995). 1994 Nine year follow-up survey (of 1985 freshmen). *Higher Education Research Institute at UCLA.* Retrieved October 18, 2010, from http://www.jstor.org/stable/3211250

Cotman, C., Carl, W., Berchtold, N., & Christie, L. A. (2007). Corrigendum: Exercise builds brain health: Key roles of growth factor cascades and inflammation. *Trends in Neurosciences, 30*(10), 489.

Crisp, B. (2007). Is it worth the effort? How feedback influences students' subsequent submission of assessable work. *Assessment & Evaluation in Higher Education, 32*(5), 571–581.

Cross, P.K. (2001) Motivation, er . . . will that be on the test? Oral presentation given to the League for Innovation in the Community College, Mission Viejo, CA

Cull, W. (2000). Untangling the benefits of multiple study opportunities and repeated testing for cued recall. *Applied Cognitive Psychology, 14*, 215–235.

Customer Service Training. McDonald's developed by 3dsolve.com. Retrieved December 12, 2010, from http://www.3dsolve.com/

Dale, E. (1969). *Audio-visual methods in teaching.* New York: Dryden.

Damasio, A. R. (1994). *Descartes' error: Emotion, reason, and the human brain.* New York: Grosset/Putnam.

Damasio, A. R. (2001). Fundamental feelings. *Nature, 413*, 781.

Davachi, L., & Bernhard, P. S. (2009). Mind the gap: Binding experiences across space and time in the human hippocampus. *Neuron, 63*(2), 267–276. doi:10.1016/j.neuron.2009.06.024

Davachi, L., Tambini, A., & Ketz, N. (2010). Enhanced brain correlations during rest are related to memory for recent experiences. *Neuron, 65*(2), 280–290.

de Byl, P. (2009). Is there an augmented reality future for e-learning? *Proceedings of the IADIS International Conference on e-Learning Algarve, Portugal 17–20 June.* Retrieved March 12, 2011, from http://www.iadisportal.org/e-learning-2009-proceedings

de Groot, A. D. (1946). *Thought and choice in chess.* Amsterdam: Noord-Hollandsche Uitgeversmaatschappij.

Dehaene, S. (2009). *Reading in the brain.* New York: Penguin Publishing.

Devlin, K. (2002). In PBS literacy links program synopses, p. 12. Retrieved February 12, 2011, from http://www.ketadultlearning.org/pdf/ged_synopses.pdf

Dewey, J. (1933). *How we think: A restatement of the relation of reflective thinking to the educative process.* Boston, MA: D.C. Heath.

Diefes-Dux, H., Follman, D., Imbrie, P.K., Zawojewski, J., Capobianco, B., & Hjalmarson, M. (2004). Model eliciting activities: An in-class approach to improving interest and persistence of women in engineering. *Proceedings of the 2004 American Society for Engineering Education Annual Conference & Exposition.* American Society for Engineering. Retrieved October 29, 2010, from http://www.iwitts.com/html/022diefes-dux.pdf

Diekelmann, S., & Born, J. (2010). Slow-wave sleep takes the leading role in memory reorganization. *Nature Reviews Neuroscience, 11,* 218. doi:10.1038/nrn2762-c2

Dondlinger, M. J. (2007). About serious games. *Journal of Applied Educational Technology, 4*(1). Retrieved January 17, 2011, from http://www.abfirstresponse.co.uk/Aybee/serious%20games.html

Donovan, M. S., Bransford, J. D., & Pellegrino, J. W. (Eds.). (1999). *How people learn: Bridging research and practice.* Washington, DC: National Academy Press.

Doyle, T. (2008). *Helping students learn in a learner centered environment: A guide to teaching in higher education.* Sterling, VA: Stylus.

Duclukovic, N. M., & Wagner, A. D. (2006). Attending to remember and remembering to attend. *Neuron, 49,* 784–787.

Duncan, N. (2007). Feed-forward: Improving students' use of tutor comments. *Assessment & Evaluation in Higher Education, 32*(3), 271–283.

Duncan, N., Prowse, S., Hughes, J., & Burke, D. (2007). Do that and I'll raise your grade: Innovative module design and recursive feedback. *Teaching in Higher Education, 12*(4), 437–445.

Dux, P. E., Ivanoff, J., Asplund, C. L. O., & Marois, R. (2006). Isolation of a central bottleneck of information processing with time-resolved fMRI. *Neuron, 52*(6), 1109–1120.

Dweck, C. S. (2006). *Mindset: The new psychology of success.* New York: Random House.

Dweck, C. (2007). In M. Krakovsky, The effort effect. *Stanford Magazine,* March/April. Retrieved September 14, 2010, from http://www.stanfordalumni.org/news/magazine/2007/marapr/features/dweck.html

Dweck, C. S. (2007). Interview in *Stanford News.* Retrieved March 11, 2011, from http://news.stanford.edu/news/2007/february7/videos/179_flash.html

Dweck, C. S. (2009). *Mindset: Powerful insights* from interview on the Positive Coaching Alliance website. Retrieved October 28, 2010, from http://www.positivecoach.org/carol-dweck.aspx

Ebbinghaus, H. (1885). *Memory: A contribution to experimental psychology.* New York: Teachers College, Columbia University.

Ebbinghaus, H. (1913). *A contribution to experimental psychology.* New York: Teachers College, Columbia University.

EDUCAUSE Learning Initiative.(2006). An Online Portfolio System for Undergraduate Engineering Students. Retrieved June 7, 2011, from http://www.edu cause.edu/ELI/ELIInnovationsImplementationsP/156786

Edwards, J., & Fraser, K. (1983). Concept maps as reflections of conceptual understanding. *Research in Science Education, 13,* 19–26.

E-Health MD. (2011). *What is AIDS?* Retrieved October 15, 2010, from http://ehealth md.com/library/aidswomen/AID_whatis.html

Eriksson, P., Perfilieva, E., Bjork-Eriksson, T., Alborn, A. M., Nordborg, C., Peterson, D., & Gage, F. H. (1998). Neurogenesis in the adult human hippocampus. *Nature Medicine, 4*(11), 1313–1317.

Ewell, P. T. (1997). *Organizing for learning: A point of entry.* Discussion proceedings at the 1997 AAHE Summer Academy Snowbird, Utah, July. National Center for Higher Education Management Systems (NCHEMS).

Examples of Authentic Assessment. Northern Illinois University. Retrieved October 5, 2010, from jove.geol.niu.edu/faculty/kitts/GEOL401/inquiryassessment401.pp

Farah, M. (2011). *Analyzing successful ways to build better brains and improve cognitive performance.* Retrieved January 3, 2011, from http://nextbigfuture.com/2011/01/ analyzing-successful-ways-to-build.html

Ferris, S. (2003). Insufficient memory: Can a pill boost your brain's ability to hold information? *Newsday.com.* Retrieved October 17, 2010, from http://www.cogni tiveliberty.org/dll/memory_drugs_newsday.html

Ferry, B., Kervin, L., Carrington, L., & Prcevich, K. (2007). The need for choice and control: Preparing the digital generation to be teachers. *ICT: Providing choices for learners and learning.* Proceedings ASCILITE Conference, Singapore. Retrieved January 12, 2011, from http://www.ascilite.org.au/conferences/singa pore07/procs/ferry.pdf

Foerde, K., Knowlton, B. J., & Poldrack, R. A. (2006). *Modulation of competing memory systems by distraction.* Retrieved January 12, 2011, from http://www.pold racklab.org/Publications/pdfs/Proc%20Natl%20Acad%20Sci%20USA%202006% 20Foerde-1.pdf

Frank, L. M., & Karlsson, M. P. (2009). Awake replay of remote experiences in the hippocampus. *Nature Neuroscience, 12*(7), 913–918.

Franklin Institute. (2004). *Early movement in animals.* Retrieved February 2011 from http://www.fi.edu/learn/brain/exercise.html

Gage, F. H., Small, S. A., Pereira, A. C., Huddleston, D.E., Brickman, A. M., Sosunov, A. A., . . . Brown, T. R. (2007). An in vivo correlate of exercise-induced neurogenesis in the adult dentate gyrus. *Proceedings of the National Academy of the Sciences of the United States of America, 104*(13), 5638–5643.

Gardiner, L. F. (1994). *Redesigning higher education: Producing dramatic gains in student learning.* Washington, DC: Graduate School of Education and Human Development, George Washington University.

Gardner, H. (1999). *Intelligence reframed: Multiple intelligences for the 21st century.* New York: Basic Books.

Gee, J. (2003). *What videogames have to teach us about learning and literacy.* New York and Houndmills, Basingstoke: Palgrave MacMillan.

Genetics Science Learning Center. (2010). University of Utah. Retrieved January 7, 2011, from http://learn.genetics.utah.edu/

Glasser, C. (1998). *The quality world series.* Chatsworth, CA: The William Glasser Institute.

Goldberg, E. (2009). *The new executive brain: Frontal lobes in a complex world.* New York: Oxford University Press.

Gould, E. (2008). In John J. Ratey, MD, *Spark: The revolutionary new science of exercise and the brain* (p. 50). New York: Little Brown.

Grabulosa, J., Serra, M., Adan, A., Falcón, C., & Bargalló, N. (2010). Glucose and caffeine effects on sustained attention: An exploratory fMRI study. *Human Psychopharmacology: Clinical and Experimental,* doi:10.1002/hup.1150.

Grasha, A. (1996). *Teaching with style.* Pittsburgh, PA: Alliance.

Gurd, V. (2009). Exercise improves learning. Trusted.MD Network. Retrieved June 10, 2011, fromhttp://trusted.md/blog/vreni_gurd/2009/04/25/exercise_improves_learning#ixzz1OtFocXfL

Hamilton, A. (2010). Studies: An Idle Brain May Be Ripe for Learning. Retrieved June, 7, 2010, from http://www.time.com/time/health/article/0,8599,1957114,00.html#ixzz1ObSMelHW

Hart, P. (2006). *How should colleges prepare students to succeed in today's global economy?* Retrieved April 24, 2010, from http://www.aacu.org/advocacy/leap/documents/Re8097abcombined.pdf

Hattie, J., & Timperley, H. (2007). The power of feedback. *Review of Educational Research, 77,* 81–112.

Herrington, J., Oliver, R., & Reeves, T. C. (2003). Patterns of engagement in authentic online learning environments. *Australian Journal of Educational Technology, 19*(1), 59–71. Retrieved April 24, 2010, from http://www.ascilite.org.au/ajet/ajet19/herrington.html

Hess, R. D. (2004). *A guide to writing scholarly articles.* Retrieved June 9, 2011, from www.elsevier.com/framework_products/ . . . /edurevReviewPaperWriting.pdf

Heuer, F., & Reisberg, D. (1990). Vivid memories of emotional events: The accuracy of remembered minutiae. *Memory & Cognition, 18,* 496–506.

Hillman, C., & Castelli, D. M. (2007a). Physically fit children appear to do better in classroom. *Research Quarterly for Exercise and Sport, 64,* 178–188.

Hillman, C. H., & Castelli, D. M. (2007b). Physical education performance outcome and cognitive function. *Journal of Sport and Exercise Psychology, 19,* 249–277.

Hillman, C. H., Castelli, D. M., Buck, S. M., & Erwin, H. (2007). Physical fitness and academic achievement in 3rd & 5th grade students. *Journal of Sport & Exercise Psychology, 29,* 239–252.

Hillman, C. H., Erickson, K., & Kramer, A. F. (2008). Be smart, exercise your heart: Exercise effects on brain and cognition. *Nature Reviews Neuroscience, 9,* 58–65. doi:10.1038/nrn2298

Hillman, C., Motl, R. W., Pontifex, M. B., Iversiteit, V., Boomsma, D., De Geus, E. J. C., Posthuma, D., & Stubbe, J. (2006). Exercise appears to improve brain function among younger people. *Science Daily.* Retrieved March 13, 2011, from http://www.sciencedaily.com/releases/2006/12/061219122200.htm

Hillman, C. H., Pontifex, M. B., Raine, L. B., Castelli, D. M., Hall, E. E., & Kramer, A. F. (2009). The effect of acute treadmill walking on cognitive control and academic achievement in preadolescent children. *Neuroscience, 159*(3), 1044–1054.

Institute of Education Sciences. (2007). *Organizing instruction and study to improve student learning.* Washington, DC: National Center for Education Research.

Isaac, J. T., Buchanan, K. A., Muller, R. U., & Mellor, J. R. (2009, May 27). Hippocampal place cell firing patterns can induce long-term synaptic plasticity in vitro. *Journal of Neuroscience, 29*(21), 6840–6850.

Jha, A. (2011). Meditation improves brain anatomy and function. *Psychiatry Research: Neuroimaging on Science Direct, 191*(1), 1–86. Retrieved January 30, 2011, from www.sciencedirect.com/science/journal/09254927

Johnson, S., & Taylor, K. (Eds.). (2006). In F. I. Editor & S. I. Editor, Functions of the human brain. *The Neuroscience of Adult Learning* (pp. 53–62). San Francisco: Jossey-Bass.

Jukes, I., & Dosa, A. J. (2003). *The InfoSavvy Group,* as quoted on www.apple.com. Retrieved November 15, 2010, from /au/education/digitalkids/disconnect/landscape.html

Kaner, S., Lind, L., Toldi, C., Fisk, S., & Berger, D. (2007). *Facilitator's guide to participatory decision-making.* San Francisco, CA: Jossey-Bass.

Karlsson M.P., & Frank L.M. (2009). Awake replay of remote experiences in the hippocampus. *Nature Neuroscience, 12*(7), 913–918.

Karp, D. A., & Yoels, W. C. (1976). The college classroom: Some observation on the meaning of student participation. *Sociology and Social Research, 60,* 421–439.

Keller, D., (2011). Academic Performance. Retrieved June 7, 2011, from http://education.jhu.edu/newhorizons/strategies/topics/applied-learning/academic-performance/

Kensinger, E. A. (2004). Remembering emotional experiences: The contribution of valence and arousal. *Reviews in the Neurosciences, 15,* 241–251.

Kerr, N. L. (1989). Illusions of efficacy: The effects of group size on perceived efficacy in social dilemmas. *Journal of Experimental Social Psychology, 25,* 287–313.

Khatri, P., Blumenthal, J. A., Babyak, M. A., Craighead, W. E., Herman, S., Baldewicz, T., Madden, D. J., . . . Krishnan, K. R. (2001). Effects of exercise training on cognitive functioning among depressed older men and women. *Journal of Aging and Physical Activity, 9,* 43–57.

Khurana, S. A collection of Alfred A. Montapert quotes. Retrieved June 7, 2011, from http://quotations.about.com/od/stillmorefamouspeople/a/AlfredAMontapeɪ.htm

Kilbourne, J. (2009). *Sharpening the mind through movement: Using exercise balls as chairs in a university class.* Retrieved October 12, 2010, from www.balldynamics.com/research/aɪ237990661.pdf

Kirschner, P. A., Sweller, J., & Clark, R. E. (2006). Why minimal guidance during instruction does not work: An analysis of the failure of constructivist, discovery, problem-based, experiential, and inquiry-based teaching. *Educational Psychologist, 41*(2), 75–86.

Klopfer, E. (2008). *Augmented learning research and design of mobile educational games.* London: The MIT Press.

Kohn, A. (1993). *Punished by rewards: The trouble with gold stars, incentive plans, A's, praise, and other bribes.* Boston, MA: Houghton Mifflin.

Kolb, D. A., & Fry, R. (1975). Toward an applied theory of experiential learning in C. Cooper (Ed.), *Theories of Group Process.* London: John Wiley.

Kramer, A. F., Hahn, S., Cohen, N. J., Banich, M. T., McAuley, E., Harrison, C. R., . . . Colcombe, A. (1999). Ageing, fitness and neurocognitive function. *Nature, 400,* 418–419.

Kramer, A. F., Voss, M. W., Ericjson, K. I., Prakash, R. S., Chaddock, L., Malkowski, E., . . . McAuley, E. (2010). Functional connectivity: A source of variance in the association between cardiorespiratory fitness and cognition? *Neuropsychologia, 48,* 1394–1406.

Kuhn, T. S. (1962). *The structure of scientific revolutions* (1st ed.). Chicago, IL: University of Chicago Press.

LaBar, K. S., & Phelps, E. A. (1998). Arousal-mediated memory consolidation: Role of the medial temporal lobe in humans. *Psychological Science, 9,* 490–493.

Larson, B. E. (2000). Classroom discussion: A method of instruction and a curriculum outcome. *Teaching and Teacher Education, 16*(5–6), 661–677.

Latane, B., & Harkins, S. G. (1998). Population and political participation: A social impact analysis of voter responsibility. *Group Dynamics, 2*(3), 192–207.

Latane, B., Williams, K., & Harkins, S. (1979). Many hands make light the work: The causes and consequences of social loafing. *Journal of Personal Sociology and Psychology, 37,* 822–832.

Lave, J. (1988). *Cognition in practice: Mind, mathematics, and culture in everyday life.* Cambridge, England: Cambridge University Press.

Lave, J., & Wenger, E. (1991). *Situated learning: Legitimate peripheral participation.* Cambridge, England: Cambridge University Press.

Lawson, L. (2002). Scaffolding as a teaching strategy. Retrieved June 7, 2011, from http://www.docstoc.com/docs/54255229/Scaffolding-as-a-Teaching-Strategy

Lepper, M., & Woolverton, M. (2002). The wisdom of practice: Lessons learned from the study of highly effective tutors. In J. Aronson (Eds.), *Improving academic achievement* (pp. 135–158). San Diego, CA: Elsevier Science.

Lepper, M. R., Woolverton, M., Mumme, D. L., & Gurtner, J. L. (1993). Motivational techniques of expert human tutors: Lessons for the design of computer-based tutors. In S. P. Lajoie & S. J. Derry (Eds.), *Computers as cognitive tool* (pp. 75–105). Hillsdale, NJ: Erlbaum.

Lesh, R. (1998). The development of representational abilities in middle school mathematics: The development of student's representations during model eliciting activities. In I. E. Sigel (Ed.), *Representations and student learning*. Mahwah, NJ: Erlbaum.

Lesh, R., Hoover, M., Hole, B., Kelly, A., & Post, T. (2000). Principles for developing thought-revealing activities for students and teachers. In A. Kelly & R. Lesh (Eds.), *Handbook of research design in mathematics and science education* (pp. 591–646). Mahwah, NJ: Lawrence Erlbaum.

Levy, F., & Murnane, R. (2005). *The new division of labor: How computers are creating the next job market*. Princeton, NJ: Princeton University Press.

Loftus, E. (2010). Explanations for forgetting: Reasons why we forget. In *about.com Psychology*. Retrieved December 13, 2010, from http://psychology.about.com/od/cognitivepsychology/tp/explanations-for-forgetting.htm

Lombardi, M. M. (2007). Authentic learning for the 21st century: An overview. *ELI Paper 1*. Retrieved November 5, 2010, from http://www.educause.edu/ELI/AuthenticLearningforthe21stCen/156769

Lowinson, J., Ruiz, P., Millman, R., & Langrod, J. (1997). *Substance abuse: A comprehensive textbook* (3rd ed.). Baltimore, MD: Williams & Wilkens.

Lowman, J. (1995). *Mastering the techniques of teaching* (2nd ed.). San Francisco, CA: Jossey-Bass.

Lwin, M. O., Morrin, W., & Krishna, A. (2010). Exploring the superadditive effects of scent and pictures on verbal recall: An extension of dual coding theory. *Journal of Consumer Psychology, 20*, 317–326.

MacKay, W. A. (1999). Neuro 101, *neurophysiology without tears* (6th ed.). Toronto, Ontario: Sefalotek.

Marra, T. (2010). *Authentic learning environments*. Retrieved November 10, 2010, from http://www-personal.umich.edu/~tmarra/authenticity/page3.html

Mattson, M. P., Duan, W., Wan, R., & Guo, Z. (2004). Prophylactic activation of neuroprotective stress response pathways by dietary and behavioral manipulations. *NeuroRx*, 111–116, Retrieved June 8, 2011, from http://www.ncbi.nlm.nih.gov/pubmed/15717011

Mayer, R. E. (1989). Systematic thinking fostered by illustrations in scientific text. *Journal of Educational Psychology, 81*, 240–246.

Mayer, R. E. (2004). Should there be a three-strikes rule against pure discovery learning? The case for guided methods of instruction. *American Psychologist, 59*(1), 14–19.

Mayer, R. E. (2009). *Multimedia learning* (2nd ed.). New York: Cambridge University Press.

Mayer, R. E., & Anderson, R. B. (1991). Animations need narrations: An experimental test of a dual-coding hypothesis. *Journal of Educational Psychology, 83,* 484–490.

Mayer, R. E., & Anderson, R. B. (1992). The instructive animation: Helping students build connections between words and pictures in multimedia learning. *Journal of Educational 84*(4), 444–452.

Mayer, R. E., & Gallini, J. K. (1990). When is an illustration worth ten thousand words? *Journal of Educational Psychology, 82,* 715–726.

Mayer, R. E., & Moreno, R. (1998a). A cognitive theory of multimedia learning: Implications for design principles. Retrieved June 8, 2011, from http://www.unm.edu/~moreno/PDFS/chi.pdf

Mayer, R. E., & Moreno, R. (1998b). A split-attention effect in multimedia learning: Evidence for dual information processing systems in working memory. *Journal of Educational Psychology, 90,* 312–320.

Mayer, R. E., & Sims, V. K. (1994). For whom is a picture worth a thousand words? Extensions of a dual-coding theory of multimedia learning. *Journal of Educational Psychology, 86,* 389–401.

Mayer, R. E., Steinhoff, K., Bower, G., & Mars, R. (1995). A generative theory of textbook design: Using annotated illustrations to foster meaningful learning of science text. *Educational Technology Research and Development, 43,* 31–44.

McAleese, R. R. (1994). A theoretical view on concept mapping. *ALT, 2*(2), 38–48.

McCabe, S. E., Knight, J. R., Teter, C. J., & Wechsler, H. (2005). Nonmedical use of prescription stimulants among U.S. college students: Prevalence and correlates from a national survey. *Addiction, 99,* 96–106.

McDaniel, M. A., & Fisher, R. P. (1991). Tests and test feedback as learning sources. *Contemporary Educational Psychology, 16,* 192–201.

McDaniel, M. A., Roediger, H. L., III, & McDermo, K. B. (2007). Generalizing test-enhanced learning from the laboratory to the classroom. *Psychonomic Bulletin & Review, 14,* 200–206.

McFarlene, A., Sparrowhawk, A., & Heald, Y. (2002). Report on the educational use of games. *Technical Report, TEEM.* Retrieved October 19, 2010, from www.teem.org.uk/publications/teem_gamesined_full.pdf

McKeachie, W. J. (1978). *Teaching tips: A guidebook for the beginning college teacher* (7th ed.). Lexington, MA: Heath.

McKeachie, W. (1994). *Teaching tips: Strategies, research, and theory for college and university teachers* (9th ed.). Lexington, MA: DC Heath.

McKenzie, J. (1999). Scaffolding for success. *The Educational Journal, (9),* 4. Retrieved November 1, 2010, from http://www.fno.org/dec99/scaffold.html

McKone, E. (1998). The decay of short-term implicit memory: Unpacking lag. *Memory and Cognition, 26*(6), 1173–1186.

Medina, J. (2008). *Brain rules*. Seattle, WA: Pear Press.

Mevarech, Z. R., & Kramarski, B. (2003). The effects of metacognitive training versus worked-out examples on students' mathematical reasoning. *British Journal of Educational Psychology, 73*, 449–471.

Michigan State University Career Services Network. *12 Essentials for success*. Retrieved October 12, 2010, from http://careernetwork.msu.edu/pdf/Competencies.pdf

Microsoft Training. (2010). *How a good smell can induce a better learning environment with PowerPoint*. Retrieved September 12, 2010, from http://www.microsofttraining.net/article-924-how-good-smell-can-induce-better-learning-environment-with-powerpoint.html

Middendorf, J., & Kalish, A. (1996). The "Change-Up" in lectures. Teaching Resources Center, Indiana University. Retrieved March 1, 2011, from http://www.ntlf.com/html/pi/9601/article1.htm

Mintzes, J. J., Wandersee, J. H., & Novak, J. D. (2000). *Assessing science understanding: A human constructivist view*. San Diego: Academic Press.

Modie, J. (2003). "Good" chemical: Neurons in brain elevated among exercise addicts. Oregon Health & Science University (September 29). *Science Daily*. Retrieved March 13, 2011, from http://www.sciencedaily.com/releases/2003/09/030929053719.htm

Mohs, R. C. (2010). *How human memory works*. Retrieved January 11, 2011, from http://health.howstuffworks.com/human-body/systems/nervous-system/human-memory4.htm

Mullen, B. (1983). Operationalizing the effect of the group on the individual: A self-attention perspective. *Journal of Experimental Social Psychology, 19*, 295–322.

Muller, J. (2006). What is authentic assessment? Retrieved June 7, 2011, from http://jfmueller.faculty.noctrl.edu/toolbox/

Najjar, L. J. (1998). Principles of educational multimedia user interface design. *Human Factors, 40*(2), 311–323.

National Library of Medicine. Visible human project. Retrieved December 12, 2010, from http://www.nlm.nih.gov/research/visible/visible_human.html

National Summit on Educational Games. (2006). *Harnessing the power of games*. Washington, DC: Federation of American Scientists.

Nauert, R. (2010). How Active Learning Improves Memory. Retrieved June 13, 2011, from http://psychcentral.com/news/2010/12/06/how-active-learning-improves-memory/21563.html

Nellis, B. (2006). Mayo clinic obesity researchers test classroom of the future. *Pediatrics/Children's Health*. Retrieved October 15, 2010, from http://www.medicalnewstoday.com/articles/39630.php

Newell, F., Bulthoff, H. H., & Ernst, M. (2003). Cross-modal perception of actively explored objects. Proceedings *EuroHaptics*, 291–299.

Newmann, F. M., Secada, W. G., & Wehlage, G. G. (1995). *A guide to authenticin-struction and assessment: Vision, standards, and scoring.* Madison, WI: Wisconsin Center for Education Research.

Nicol, D., & Draper, S. (2008). Redesigning written feedback to students when class sizes are large. Paper presented at the *Improving University Teachers Conference*, July, Glasgow.

Nidich, S. I., Fields, J. Z., Rainforth, M. V., Pomerantz, R., Cella, D., Kristeller J., & Schneider, R.H. (2009). A Randomized controlled trial of the effects of transcendental meditation on quality of life in older breast cancer patients. *Integrative Cancer Therapies, 8*(3), 228–234.

Nilson, L. (1996). *Teaching at its best.* Nashville, TN: Vanderbilt University.

North Central Regional Education Laboratory. (2011). *Traits of Authentic Education.* Retrieved October 14, 2010, from www.ncrel.org/sdrs/areas/issues/content/cntar-eas/science/sc500.ht m

Novak, J. D. (1990). Concept maps and vee diagrams: Two metacognitive tools for science and mathematics education. *Instructional Science, 19*, 29–52.

Novak, J. D., & Cañas, A. J. (2006). *The theory underlying concept maps and how to construct and use them.* Retrieved December 7, 2010, from http://cmap.ihmc.us/ Publications/ResearchPapers/TheoryCmaps/TheoryUnderlyingConceptMaps.htm

Novak, J. D., & Gowin, D. B. (1984). *Learning how to learn.* New York: Cambridge University Press.

Oberlander, E. M., Oswald, F. L., Hambrick, D. Z., & Jones, L. A. (2007). Individual differences as predictors of error during multitasking. *Technical Report for Navy Personnel Research, Studies, and Technology* (NPRST-TN-07-9). Millington, TN.

Ochsner, K. N. (2000). Are affective events richly recollected or simply familiar? The experience and process of recognizing feelings past. *Journal of Experimental Psychology: General, 129*, 242–261.

Orts, E. W. (2010). *Tragedy of the Tuna.* Retrieved December 12, 2010, from http:// www.wharton.upenn.edu/learning/tragedy-of-the-tuna.cfm

Overbaugh, R., & Schultz, L. (2008). Blooms Revised Taxonomy Comparison. Retrieved June 9, 2011, from http://www.odu.edu/educ/roverbau/Bloom/ blooms_taxonomy.htm

Paivio, A. (1986). *Mental representations: A dual coding approach.* Oxford, England: Oxford University Press.

Pashler, H., Bain, P., Bottge, B., Graesser, A., Koedinger, K., McDaniel, M., & Metcalfe, J. (2007). *Organizing instruction and study to improve student learning* (NCER 2007-2004). Washington, DC: National Center for Education Research, Institute of Education Sciences, U.S. Department of Education.

Pashler, H., Cepeda, N., Wixted, J., & Rohrer, D. (2005). When does feedback facilitate learning of words? *Journal of Experimental Psychology: Learning, Memory, and Cognition, 31*, 3–8.

Pashler, H., Rohrer, D., Cepeda, N. J., & Carpenter, S. K. (2007). Enhancing learning and retarding forgetting: Choices and consequences. *Psychonomic Bulletin and Review, 14*, 187–193.

Perry, D. J. (2002). *Unit 5: Cognitive development theories.* Retrieved November 16, 2010, from http://www.education.indiana.edu/~p540/webcourse/develop.html

Pert, C. B. (1997). *Molecules of emotion: The science behind mind-body medicine.* New York: Simon & Schuster.

Piaget, J. (1954). *The construction of reality in the child.* New York: Basic Books.

Piezon, S. L., & Donaldson, R. L. (2005). Online groups and social loafing: Understanding student-group interactions. *Online Journal of Distance Learning Administration, 8*(4). Retrieved July 7, 2010, from http://www.westga.edu/~distance/ojdla/winter84/piezon84.htm

Prensky, M. (2001). *What readers are saying about digital game-based learning.* New York: McGraw-Hill.

Price, K. H., & Harrison, D. A. (2006). Withholding inputs in team context: Member composition, interaction process, evaluation structure, and social loafing. *Journal of Applied Psychology, 91*(6), 444–452.

Pytel, B. (2007). No more classroom chairs, students are sitting on exercise balls. *Suite101.com.* Retrieved November 11, 2010, from http://www.balldynamics.com/research/a1235761967.pdf

Rasch, B., Buchel, C., Gais, S., & Born, J. (2007, March 9). Odor cues during slow wave sleep prompt declarative memory consolidation. *Science,* 1426–1429.

Ratey, J. (2001). *A user's guide to the brain.* New York: Pantheon Books.

Ratey, J. (2008). *Spark: The revolutionary new science of exercise and the brain.* New York: Little Brown.

Rawson, K. (2010). Practice tests really do improve learning. *The Journal Science Practice.* Retrieved November 1, 2010, from http://health.usnews.com/health-news/family-health/brain-and-behavior/articles/2010/10/14/practice-tests-really-do-improve-learning-study.html

Resnick, L. B. (1987). The 1987 Presidential Address: Learning in school and out. *Educational Researcher, 16*(9), 13–20.

Ribeiro, S. (2004). Sleeper effects: Slumber may fortify memory, stir insight. *Science News, 165*(4), 53.

Ribeiro, S., Gervasoni, D., Soares, E. S., Zhou, Y., Lin, S. C., Pantoja, J., Lavine, M., & Nicolelis, M. A. (2004). Long-lasting novelty-induced neuronal reverberation during slow-wave sleep in multiple forebrain areas. *PLoS Biology, 2*(1), 24. doi:10.1371/journal.pbio.0020024.

Rinck, M. (1999). Memory for everyday objects: Where are the digits on numerical keypads? *Applied Cognitive Psychology, 13*(4), 329–350.

Robert, B. C. (2000). Patterns, the brain, and learning. *The Science of Learning, 4*(3).

Roediger, H. L., III, & Karpicke, J. D. (2006). *The power of testing memory: Implications for educational practice.* Unpublished manuscript, Washington University in St. Louis.

Rogers, D., Deno, S. L., & Markell, M. (2001). Systematic Teaching and Recording Tactic S.T.A.R.T.: A generic reading strategy. *Intervention, 37*(2), 96–100.

Rogers, S., Ludington, J., & Graham, S. (1998). *Motivation and learning.* Evergreen, CO: Peak Learning Systems.

Rogers, S., & Renard, L. (1999). Relationship-driven teaching. *Educational Leadership.* September, 34–37.

Ruggerio, V. (1995). Oral presentation on *Thinking Critically,* given at Ferris State University, March 1995.

Rule, A. C. (2006). Editorial: The components of authentic learning. *Journal of Authentic Learning, 3*(1), 1–10.

Sahakian, B., & Morein-Zamir, S. (2007). Professor's little helper. *Nature, 450,* 1157–1159. Retrieved December 7, 2010, from http://www.nature.com/nature/journal/v450/n7173/full/4501157a.html

San Francisco Edit. (2010). *Research related questions.* Retrieved October 11, 2010, http://www.sfedit.net/index.html

Schacter, D. (2001). *The seven sins of memory: How the mind forgets and remembers.* Boston, MA: Houghton Mifflin.

Schacter, D. L., & Dodson, C. S. (2001, September 29). Misattribution, false recognition and the sins of memory. *Philosophical Transactions of the Royal Society of London B: Biological Sciences, 356*(1413), 1385–1393. doi: 10.1098/rstb.2001.0938

Schwarz, R. (2002). *The skilled facilitator: A comprehensive resource for consultants, facilitators, managers, trainers, and coaches.* San Francisco, CA: Jossey-Bass.

Seitz, A. R., Kim, R., & Shams, L. (2006). Sound facilitates visual learning. *Current Biology, 16*(14) 1422–1427.

Serra-Grabulosa, J., Adan, A., Falcón, C., & Bargalló, N. (2010). Glucose and caffeine effects on sustained attention: An exploratory fMRI study. *Human Psychopharmacology: Clinical and Experimental, 25*(7–8), 543–552.

Shams, L., & Seitz, A. (2008). Benefits of multisensory learning. *Trends in Cognitive Science, 12*(11), 411–417.

Shankardass, A. (2009). *A second opinion on learning disorders* (TED). Retrieved September 9, 2010, from http://www.ted.com/talks/aditi_shankardass_a_second_opinion_on_learning_disorders.html

Simon, P. (1966). I am a Rock, I am an Island [Simon & Garfunkel]. *Simon & Garfunkel Collected Works* [LP]. New York: Columbia Records.

Smagorinsky, P. (2007). Vygotsky and the social dynamic of classrooms. *English Journal, 97*(2), 61–66.

Smallwood, J., & Schooler, J. (2006). The restless mind. *Psychological Bulletin, 132*(6), 946–958.

Smith, C. N., & Squire, L. R. (2009). Medial temporal lobe activity during retrieval of semantic memory is related to the age of the memory. *The Journal of Neuroscience, January 28, 29*(4), 930–938. doi:10.1523/JNEUROSCI.4545-08

Smith, F. (1985). *Reading without nonsense.* New York: Teacher College Press.

Smith, M. K. (2001). Facilitating learning and change in groups. *The Encyclopedia of Informal Education.* Retrieved October 17, 2010, from http://www.infed.org/encyclopedia.htm

Soanes, C., Stevenson, A., & Hawker, S. (2006). *Concise Oxford English dictionary (computer software)* (11th ed.). Oxford, England: Oxford University Press.

Spiller, D. (2009). *Assessment: Feedback to promote student learning.* Retrieved November 1, 2010, from http://www.docstoc.com/docs/24436889/Assessment-Feedback-to-promote-student-learning

Staresina, B. P., & Davachi, L. (2009). Mind the gap: Binding experiences across space and time in the human hippocampus. *Neuron, 63*(2), 267–276.

Stark, L. A. (2010). *The new science of addiction.* Genetics Science Learning Center, University of Utah. Retrieved October 4, 2010, from http://learn.genetics.utah.edu/units/addition/index.cfm

Stenberg, G. (2006). Conceptual and perceptual factors in the picture superiority effect. *The European Journal of Cognitive Psychology, 18*(6), 813–847.

Stern, Y. (2009). Cognitive reserve. *Neuropsychologia, 47,* 2015–2028.

Sweller, J. (1988). Cognitive load during problem solving: Effects on learning. *Cognitive Science, 12,* 257–285.

Sweller, J., Kirschner, P. A., & Clark, R. E. (2007). Why minimally guided teaching techniques do not work: A reply to commentaries. *Educational Psychologist, 42*(2), 115–121.

Swing, E. L., Gentile, D. A., Anderson, C. A., & Walsh, D. A. (2010). Television and video game exposure and the development of attention problems. *Pediatrics,* doi:10.1542/peds.2009-1508

Sylwester, R. (1995). *A celebration of neurons: An educator's guide to the human brain.* Alexandria, VA: Association for Supervision and Curriculum Development.

Tambini, A., Ketz, N., & Davachi, L. (2010, January). Enhanced brain correlations during rest are related to memory for recent experiences. *Neuron, 65*(2), 280–290.

Taras, M. (2003). To feedback or not to feedback in student self-assessment. *Assessment and Evaluation in Higher Education, 28*(5), 549–565.

Taylor, D. (2009). Modern myths of learning: The creative right brain. *Training Zone.* Retrieved February 19, 2011, from http://donaldhtaylor.wordpress.com/writing/modern-myths-of-learning-the-creative-right-brain/

Thompson, C. J. (2009).Educational Statistics Authentic Learning CAPSULES: Community action projects for students utilizing leadership and e-based statistics. *Journal of Statistics Education,* Retrieved June 8, 2011, from http://www.amstat.org/publications/jse/v17n1/thompson.htm

Thompson, D. (2006). *Summit on educational games: Harnessing the power of video games for learning.* Washington, DC: Federation of American Scientist. Retrieved

December 7, 2010, from http://www.adobe.com/resources/elearning/pdfs/serious_games_wp.pdf

UNC Center for Teaching and Learning. (1992). *The guided discussion: Ground rules for in-class small group discussion, for your consideration . . . Suggestions and reflections on teaching and learning*, CTL Number 12. Retrieved February 19, 2011, from http://cfe.unc.edu/pdfs/FYC12.pdf

Underwood, B. J., & Postman, L. (1960). Extra-experimental sources of interference in forgetting. *Psychological Review, 67,* 73–95.

U.S. Bureau of Labor Statistics. (2008). Number of jobs, labor market experience, and earnings growth: Results from a national longitudinal survey news release, June 2008. Retrieved November 18, 2010, from http://www.bls.gov/news.release/archives/nlsoy_06272008.htm

U.S. Department of Education. (2001). *The National Commission of the High School Senior Year.* Retrieved January 12, 2010, from http://www.ecs.org/html/Document.asp?chouseid=2929

U.S. Department of Labor. (2008). Number of Jobs Help from 18–42. Retrieved June 10, 2011, from http://www.bls.gov/nls/y79r22jobsbyedu.pdf

Voss, J. L., Gonsalves, B. D., Federmeier, K. D., Tranel, D., & Cohen N. J. (2011, January). Hippocampal brain-network coordination during volitional exploratory behavior enhances learning. *Nature Neuroscience, 14*(1), 115–120.

Walker, M.P. (2009). The role of slow wave sleep in memory processing. *Journal of Clinical Sleep Medicine, 5,* S20–S26.

Weimer, M. (2002). *Learner-centered teaching.* San Francisco, CA: Jossey-Bass.

Weuve, J., Kang, J., Manson, J., Breteler, M., Ware, J., & Grodstein, F. (2008). Physical activity, including walking, and cognitive function in older women. Retrieved January 23, 2011, from http://jama.ama-assn.org/content/292/12/1454.abstract

Whitebread, D. (1997). Developing children's problem-solving: The educational uses of adventure games. In A. McFarlane (Ed.), *Information technology and authentic learning* (pp. 13–39). London: Routledge.

Whitson, J., & Galinsky, A. (2008). Lacking control increases illusory pattern perception. *Science, 322*(5898), 115–117.

Wiggins, G. (1990). The case for authentic assessment. *Practical Assessment, Research & Evaluation, 2*(2). Retrieved March 8, 2011, from http://PAREonline.net/getvn.asp?v=2&n=

Wiggins, G. (2004). *Assessment as Feedback.* New Horizons for Learning: Johns Hopkins University School of Education. Retrieved February 14, 2011, from http://education.jhu.edu/newhorizons/strategies/topics/Assessment%20Alternatives/wiggins.htm

Williams, M. (2005). A technology-based model for learning. *Journal on Systemics, Cybernetics, and Informatics.* Retrieved June 8, 2011, from http://www.iiisci.org/journal/CV$/sci/pdfs/P355312.pdf

Yambric, W. (2008). A scaffolding approach to teaching calculus in high school: Conversation at parent–teachers conference, Big Rapids High School.

Ying, Z., Vaynman, S., & Gomez-Pinilla, F. (2004). Exercise induces BDNF and synapses to specific hippocampal subfields. *Journal of Neuroscientific Research, 76*(3), 356–362.

Zadina, J. (2010). *Neuroscience and learning.* Oral presentation at San Jacinto Community College, Houston, TX.

Zins, J. E., Wang, M. C., Weissberg, R. P., & Walberg, H. J. (2004). *Building academic success on social and emotional learning: What does the research say?* New York: Teachers College Press.

Zull, J. (2002). *The art of changing the brain.* Sterling, VA: Stylus.

Also available from Stylus

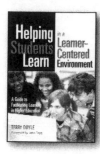

Helping Students Learn in a Learner-Centered Environment
A Guide to Facilitating Learning in Higher Education
Terry Doyle
Foreword by John Tagg

"Doyle offers a great deal of practical advice on how to prepare students to engage in student-centered learning activities . . . the book contains many useful tips as well as appendices which provide rubrics and other helpful resources."—*Teaching Theology and Religion*

"Oh boy, am I glad this book is here. Terry Doyle has explored and integrated a wide range of literature on learning. His book brings together findings that will enable us to answer what so many college & university faculty members want to know: How do we enable our students to learn to learn (and love it)? If your goal is to develop lifelong learners, this book is a guidebook for your practice."—*Laurie Richlin*

Before entering higher education, most students' learning experiences have been traditional and teacher-centered. Their teachers have typically controlled their learning, with students having had little say about what and how to learn. For many students, encountering a learner-centered environment will be new, possibly unsettling, and may even engender resistance and hostility.

Taking as his starting point students' attitudes toward, and unfamiliarity with, learner-centered classrooms, Terry Doyle explains that motivating students to engage with this practice first of all requires explaining its underlying rationale, and then providing guidance on how to learn in this environment. This book is about how to help students acquire the new skills and knowledge they need to take on unfamiliar roles and responsibilities. It is informed by the author's extensive experience in managing learner-centered classes, and by his consultation work with faculty.

Two books by James E. Zull

The Art of Changing the Brain
Enriching the Practice of Teaching by Exploring the Biology of Learning
James E. Zull

"This is the best book I have read about the brain and learning. Zull takes us on a fascinating and vivid tour of the brain, revealing the intricate structure of the organ designed by evolution to learn from experience. Using wonderful stories from his own experience, filled with insight, humor, and occasional twinges of pain, this wise and humane educator and scientist describes his concept that teaching is the art of changing the brain. His perspective forms the foundation for a teaching approach that can dramatically improve human learning."—*David A. Kolb*, *Dept. of Organizational Behavior, Case Western Reserve University*

James Zull invites teachers in higher education or any other setting to accompany him in his exploration of what scientists can tell us about the brain and to discover how this knowledge can influence the practice of teaching. He describes the brain in clear non-technical language and an engaging conversational tone, highlighting its functions and parts and how they interact, and always relating them to the real world of the classroom and his own evolution as a teacher.

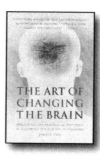

From Brain to Mind
Using Neuroscience to Guide Change in Education
James E. Zull

"My congratulations to James Zull for the way he connects neuroscience and education, and offers valuable insights on how we can be more intentional in improving the opportunities and conditions for learning in and out of the classroom. This book is articulate, and convincing, and strikes an excellent balance between a substantive explication of brain science and an engaging and conversational style."—*Elkhonon Goldberg*, *Clinical Professor of Neurology at the NYU School of Medicine, author of* The New Executive Brain

Stating that educational change is underway and that the time is ripe to recognize that "the primary objective of education is to understand human learning" and that "all other objectives depend on achieving this understanding", James Zull challenges the reader to focus on this purpose, first for her or himself, and then for those for whose learning they are responsible.

The book is addressed to all learners and educators—to the reader as self-educator embarked on the journey of lifelong learning, to the reader as parent, and to readers who are educators in schools or university settings, as well as mentors and trainers in the workplace.

In this work, James Zull presents cognitive development as a journey taken by the brain, from an organ of organized cells, blood vessels, and chemicals at birth, through its shaping by experience and environment into potentially to the most powerful and exquisite force in the universe, the human mind.

At a time when we can expect to change jobs and careers frequently during our lifetime, when technology is changing society at break-neck speed, and we have instant access to almost infinite information and opinion, he argues that self-knowledge, awareness of how and why we think as we do, and the ability to adapt and learn, are critical to our survival as individuals; and that the transformation of education, in the light of all this and what neuroscience can tell us, is a key element in future development of healthy and productive societies.

22883 Quicksilver Drive
Sterling, VA 20166-2102

Subscribe to our e-mail alerts: www.Styluspub.com